Y0-BYM-758

THE CAMBRIDGE ANCIENT HISTORY

EDITORS

Volumes I–VI

J. B. BURY, M.A., F.B.A.

S. A. COOK, LITT.D.

F. E. ADCOCK, M.A., F.B.A.

Volumes VII–XI

S. A. COOK, LITT.D., F.B.A.

F. E. ADCOCK, M.A., F.B.A.

M. P. CHARLESWORTH, M.A.

Volume XII

S. A. COOK, LITT.D., F.B.A.

F. E. ADCOCK, M.A., F.B.A.

M. P. CHARLESWORTH, M.A.

N. H. BAYNES, M.A., F.B.A.

FIFTH VOLUME OF PLATES

CAMBRIDGE
UNIVERSITY PRESS
LONDON: BENTLEY HOUSE
NEW YORK, TORONTO, BOMBAY
CALCUTTA, MADRAS: MACMILLAN
TOKYO: MARUZEN COMPANY LTD

THE
CAMBRIDGE
ANCIENT HISTORY

EDITED BY

S. A. COOK, Litt. D., F.B.A.

F. E. ADCOCK, M.A., F.B.A.

M. P. CHARLESWORTH, M.A.

N. H. BAYNES, M.A., F.B.A.

VOLUME OF PLATES V

PREPARED BY

C. T. SELTMAN, M.A.

CAMBRIDGE
AT THE UNIVERSITY PRESS
1939

1809

PRINTED IN GREAT BRITAIN

PREFACE

The fifth and last volume of plates serves to illustrate a variety of monuments which have been referred to in Volumes XI and XII of the *Cambridge Ancient History*. The surviving mass of antiquities that was created between the foundation of the first and the rise of the second Flavian Dynasties is so great, scattered as it is from Scotland to Arabia and from Spain to Chinese Turkestan, that a rigorous selection of illustrations has been enforced by limitation of space. Enough should, however, be found here to give a general impression of the flow of art during nearly three centuries. From Vespasian to Commodus that Graeco-Roman art-stream, which the fourth volume of plates showed in process of formation, continued to spread over the world, so that there were men who could drink from Campanian silver cups in Sweden and seal with Greek intaglios in Khotan. With the advent of the Severan Dynasty there was a change.

Juvenal's complaint, *iam pridem Syrus in Tiberim defluxit Orontes*, was an exaggeration for his day and certainly untrue of the art of his time. But it was an unconscious prophecy.

The Syrians, Domna, Maesa and Mamaea, Caracalla posing as the new Alexander, and Elagabalus with his curious cult, all poured into Italy a flood of oriental ideas which presently had a far more profound effect on art than on politics or economics. Classical realism is seen gradually giving place to eastern expressionism until there arises the new dynamic simplification that concentrates on strength of expression. This is the late-classical art that was to lead to the art called Byzantine.

In architecture this volume, which includes buildings from the Colosseum to the Basilica of Maxentius, illustrates the most imposing achievements of the architects of Rome as well as some of the finest buildings of the Empire.

The volume is indebted to the writers of the several chapters concerned for the selection of the subjects illustrated and for the commentaries. Dr Ekholm has dealt with the objects found in the lands of the Northern Peoples, Professor Rostovtzeff with those of Sarmatians and Parthians, and Professor Alföldi with finds in the Danubian region. Spanish and African antiquities are described by Professor Albertini, British by Professor Collingwood, and Rhenish by Dr Stade. Professor Halphen has supervised the description of the Central Asian monuments, and Professor Nock of those illustrating the pagan cults of the Empire, while Professor Christensen has dealt with the early Sassanid antiquities. I am responsible for a few isolated plates, and, as formerly, for the description of coins which have been referred to by the writers of many chapters. In the period covered by the two last volumes of the *Cambridge Ancient History* the evidential value of coins is so considerable that it has seemed desirable to illustrate a fairly large number. The chief contributor to this volume is Professor Rodenwaldt, whose expert selection of illustrations and careful commentaries on no less than sixty plates tell the story of the gradual change in the art of the ancient world and lead up to the splendours of the age of Constantine.

The Editors wish to join Professor Rodenwaldt in expressing gratitude to the Directors of the German Institutes in Athens and Rome for their help in providing photographs, and especially to Mr A. D. Trendall for much time spent in securing illustrations required for this volume when he was Librarian of the British School in Rome.

Thanks for assistance in supplying photographs are due to the Director of the British Museum and to the Directors and Curators of museums in Berlin, Bonn, Budapest, Cassel, Cluj, Copenhagen, Mainz, Mannheim, New York, Schwerin, Stettin and Trèves, also to the German Archaeological Institute in Berlin, to the Departments of Antiquities in Algeria, Tunisia and Syria, to the Yale Doura Expedition in New Haven, and to Mademoiselle Brühl of the Musée Guimet in Paris. Acknowledgement is gratefully made to Professor A. B. Cook for the loan of certain blocks from his *Zeus*, and to Professor Albertini, Professor J. Kostrzewski, Mr R. P. Longden, Herr J. Rodenwaldt, Professor Rostovtzeff, Monsieur H. Seyrig, Dr E. M. W. Tillyard, and Dr N. Toll for the use of photographs in their possession.

PREFACE

Help in providing plaster casts of coins has been given by **Mr J. Allen** and **Mr H.** Mattingly of the British Museum, by Monsieur J. Babelon of the Bibliothèque Nationale in Paris, by **Mr G.** Galster of the Royal Cabinet in Copenhagen, and by the Director of the Münzkabinett in Berlin, and thanks are due to all of them. Mrs Collingwood, Miss M. V. Taylor, and Mr Martin Robertson have kindly rendered help in various ways.

Reproductions from the books specified have been sanctioned by the following publishers:

J. Bard, Berlin (Delbrueck, *Bildnisse römischer Kaiser*).

F. Bruckmann A.-G., Munich (Brunn, *Denkmäler*; Herrmann, *Denkmäler der Malerei*).

The Clarendon Press, Oxford (Collingwood, *Roman Britain*; Rostovtzeff, *Animal Style in South Russia and China*; id. *Caravan Cities*; id. *Economic and Social History of the Roman Empire*; id. *Iranians and Greeks in South Russia*; Stein, *Ancient Khotan*).

W. de Gruyter and Co., Berlin (*Die Antike*; *Baalbek*; Delbrueck, *Antike Porphyrwerke*; id. *Spätantike Kaiserporträts*; Ebert, *Reallexikon der Vorgeschichte*; Schede, *Griechische und römische Skulptur, Istanbul*).

Fischer and Franke, Berlin (Noack, *Baukunst*).

A. Fontemoing, Paris (Gsell, *Les Monuments antiques de l'Algérie*).

P. Geuthner, Paris (*Syria*; Cumont, *Fouilles de Doura-Europos*; id. *Religions orientales dans le Paganisme Romain*).

U. Hoepli, Milan (*Monumenti Antichi*; *Notizie degli Scavi*).

M. Hürlimann, Zürich (*Das Mittelmeer*).

Imprimeries Réunies, Paris (Dieulafoy, *L'Art antique en Perse*).

Istituto d' Arti Grafiche, Bergamo (*Africa Italiana*).

A. Marcus and E. Weber, Bonn (Delbrueck, *Antike Porträts*).

Propyläen-Verlag, Berlin (Rodenwaldt, *Die Kunst der Antike*).

D. Reimer and E. Vohsen, Berlin (Herzfeld, *Am Tor von Asien*).

G. Reimer, Berlin (Cichorius, *Die Reliefs der Trajanssäule*).

E. Wasmuth, Berlin (Hielscher, *Das unbekannte Spanien*; Sarre and Herzfeld, *Iranische Felsreliefs*).

The Staff of the University Press once again deserve thanks for their skill and labour in dealing with a volume that it has been no easy task to produce. In concluding the last volume of plates, I wish to record my deep indebtedness and gratitude to the Editors of the *History* for their advice and help during fourteen years of co-operation.

PREFACE

There is a design on the outside cover after a second-century bronze statuette, in the possession of Professor A. B. Cook, representing a syncretism of several goddesses. The figure is robed as Venus, has the horns of Io or Hathor, the plumes of Isis, a pillar like that of Athena Parthenos, and the rudder and cornucopiae of Tyche.

C.T.S.

December 1938

TABLE OF CONTENTS

ix

CONTENTS

CONTENTS

CONTENTS

xii

CONTENTS

CONTENTS

[a]

[b]

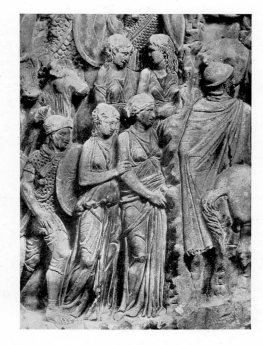

[c]

THE NORTHERN PEOPLES

This and the following pages (6, 8, 10, 12, 18, 20) show side by side objects of native manufacture and imports from the Roman Empire.

BOHEMIA

[*a*] Two Roman bronze trullae with strainers.

[*b*] Bronze buckle.

[*c*] Roman gold pendant.

[*d*] Roman bronze trulla.

[*e*] Handle of Roman bronze jug.

[*f*] Bronze mounts for a drinking horn.

[*g*] Celtic bronze fibula.

[*h*], [*i*] Native bronze fibulae.

[*j*] Bronze buckle, Roman Provincial type.

[*k*] Iron sword, bent before burial.

[*l*] Bronze fibula.

[*m*] Roman bucket (*situla*).

[*n*] Iron spearhead.

[*o*] Iron head of javelin.

[*p*] Native potting vessel.

[*g*], [*j*], [*l*], [*m*]–[*o*] from the cemetery of *Pičhora* near *Dobřichov*. (xi, 57, 70.)

[After A. Stocký, *La Bohême à l'âge du fer*, Prague, 1933]

4

GERMANY

[*a*] West-Germanic earthern vessel with 'Rädchenmäander.' (xi, 60.)

[*b*] Bronze fibula.

[*c*], [*f*] Bronze buckles.

[*d*] Bone comb.

[*e*] Burgundian iron girdle-hook. (xi, 61.)

[*g*] Gold clasp for a woman's necklace.

[*h*] Roman silver cup.

[*i*] Gold pendant for a woman's necklace.

[*j*] Silver fibula.

[*k*] Bronze strap-end.

[*l*] Roman silver bowl.

[*m*] Bronze buckle.

[*n*] Bronze armlet.

[*o*] East-Germanic earthen vessel with 'Linienbandmäander.' (xi, 60.)

Except [*c*] and [*h*] all native work. (xi, 70, 72.)

[*a*]–[*d*], [*f*] and [*l*] from West-Germanic territory; the rest from East-Germanic; [*l*] comes from the great silver hoard of *Hildesheim* (E. Pernice and F. Winter, *Der Hildesheimer Silberfund*, Berlin, 1901); [*e*] from the Burgundian burial-place at *Ramhütte, Pomerania* (J. Kostrzewski, *Die ostgermanische Kultur der Spätlatènezeit*, Mannus-Bibliothek, xviii, 1919, Abb. 43); [*h*] is from a burial at *Lübzow, Pomerania* (*Praehist. Zeitschr.* 1912); [*j*] from a burial at *Rondsen* (S. Anger, *Das Gräberfeld von Rondsen*, Graudenz, 1890).

[a] [b] [c] [d] [e] [f] [g] [h] [i] [j] [k] [l] [m] [n] [o]

DENMARK

Objects from inhumation graves. [a] Silver cup signed by a Greek silversmith and made in Capua. (xi, 61, 63.) For similar cups see Volume of Plates, iv, 128.

[b], [c] Silver hairpins with heads covered in filigree decorated gold leaf.

[d] Bowl of bluish-white glass of a type common in Pompeii. (xi, 61, 63.)

[e], [f] Silver fibula with gold-wire ornament.

[g] Glass beaker with facet surface. A similar piece has been found in Pompeii. (xi, 61, 63.)

[h] Pottery from a typical Jutland inhumation burial.

All except [a], [d] and [g] are of native workmanship. (xi, 70, 72.)

[a], [e], [f] from *Hoby, Laaland* (*Nordiske Fortidsminder*, ii, 3, pl. VIII and figs. 33, 35); [d] *Espe, Fyn* (*Aarbøger f. nord. Oldkynd.* 1871, p. 448); [b], [c], [g] *Juellinge, Laaland* (*Nordiske Fortidsminder*, ii, 1, pl. III 8, II 2); [h] *Ryomgaard, Jutland* (*Aarbøger f. nord. Oldkynd.* 1915, p. 153).

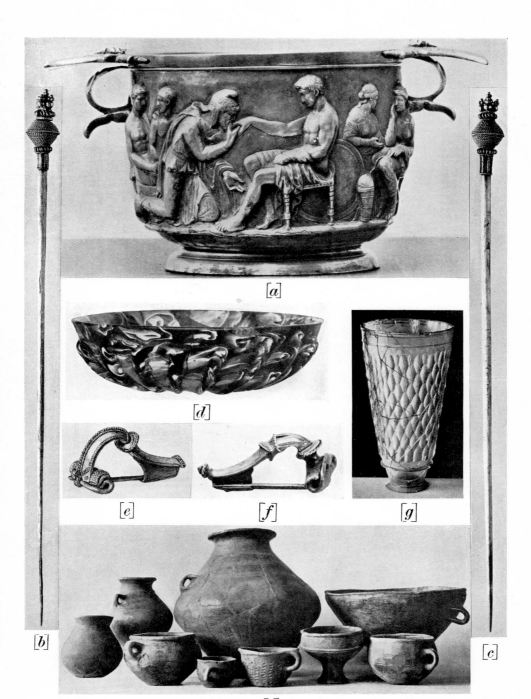

[a]

[b]

[c]

[d]

[e]

[f]

[g]

[h]

THE NORTHERN PEOPLES

THE SCANDINAVIAN PENINSULA

Objects from graves and other finds. [a] Gold pendant with filigree work from a necklace (cf. p. 6 [i]).

[b], [c] Silver coins of Verus and Faustina Junior. Of some 7000 Roman coins from Scandinavian lands more than 5000 have been found in the island of Gotland. (xi, 61.)

[d], [f] Gold finger-rings; these, which were perhaps wedding-rings, were worn on the right hand by men and women.

[e] Iron shield-boss with small round and ornamental silver plates, bronze rivets, and handle with rivets. The rivets on boss and handle have silver-plated heads. The profiled ends of the handle are decorated with filigree silver foil and small dummy silver rivet heads.

[g] Iron sword, with one edge. (xi, 58.)

[h] Bronze strap-end.

[i], [k], [l] Silver fibulae with gold filigree work.

[j] Pottery bowl.

[m], [o] Glass gaming pieces. (xi, 61, 71.)

[n] Bone die.

[p] Gold pendant resembling [a] but older.

All except [b], [c], [m], [o] of native workmanship (xi, 70, 72 *sq.*).

[a]–[c], [e], [h], [j], [m]–[o] found in Sweden, the rest in Norway. [a], [e], [h] from *Öland*; [b], [c] *Skåne*; [d], [f], [i], [l] from a woman's skeleton in the cemetery at *Store-Dal, Østfold* (see pp. 12, 14); [g] *Hedmark*; [j] *Gotland*; [m]–[o] *Östergötland*; [k] *Østfold*; [p] *Vestfold*.

10

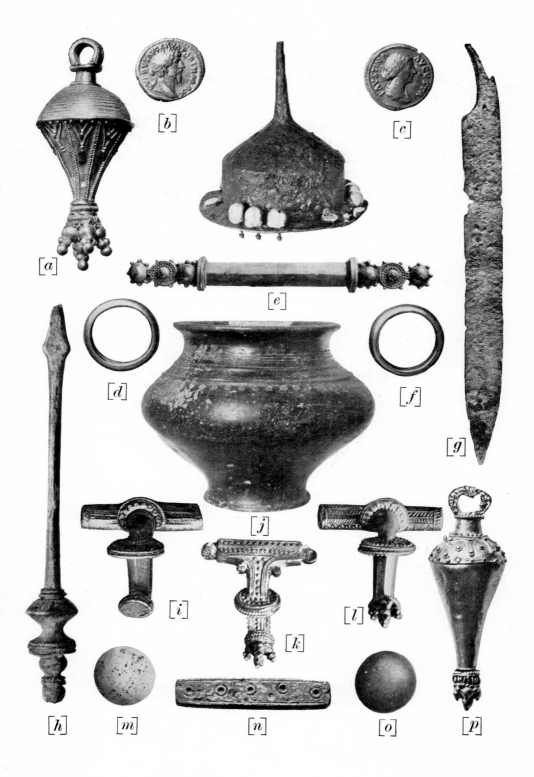

[a] [b] [c]

[d] [e] [f]

[g]

[h] [i] [j] [k] [l]

[m] [n] [o] [p]

BURIAL CUSTOMS

According to Tacitus the Germanic peoples cremated their dead and their burial customs were simple. These statements are too definite. From the late Bronze age onwards cremation was the more common, but through Celtic influence inhumation occasionally came into use before our era, and later became frequent. At this time Roman bronze and glass ware frequently appears, especially in inhumation graves. The older hypothesis, that such graves contained the remains of Roman traders, has long been abandoned. The numerous fibulae, the majority of the pottery, etc. are local work, and, furthermore, these richly equipped tombs are typically barbarian and un-Roman. (xi, 72 *sq.*)

[*a*] Part of the contents of an inhumation grave at *Grossgrünow, Pomerania. Terra sigillata* bowl, Roman bronze jug and local pottery bowl.

[*Mannus, Ergbd.* v, Taf. XVI]

[*b*] Detail of a woman's grave at *Juellinge, Laaland, Denmark.* At the shoulders silver fibulae, on the skull gold and silver hair pins [see p. 8 [*b*], [*c*], on the fingers rings, in the hand strainer for a trulla, above the head scissors, glass cups, drinking horns, lock and key of a wooden box, trulla and a damaged bronze cauldron.

[*Nordiske Fortidsminder*, ii, pl. 1]

[*c*] Grave with cremation burial from the cemetery at *Store-Dal, Østfold, Norway.* Bronze bowl containing a trulla and two glass bowls; above fragment of a bronze cauldron.

[*Norske Oldfund*, i, 1923, fig. on p. 41]

[a]

[b]

[c]

BURIALS

Tacitus declared that the Germanic peoples buried their dead in barrows. Archaeological research has, however, proved that barrow-burials do not predominate, for both low stone cairns and flat tomb-stones of various shapes, circular, triangular, or rectangular, were generally employed. A further type, common in cemeteries both in the island of Bornholm and in Sweden and Norway, was that of the Standing Stones (Swedish *bautastenar*) usually erected on level ground. In Denmark and Germany most of those inhumation graves that are rich in Roman imports are without any exterior mark or monument which would merely have been an invitation to grave-robbers. (xi, 63).

[a] Standing stones in the cemetery at *Gödåker* in *Uppland, Sweden.*

[b] A view of the *Store-Dal* cemetery in *Østfold, Norway.*

[From *Fornvännen*, 20, 1925, p. 326, and from *Norske Oldfund*, ɪ, 1923, fig. on p. 4]

[a]

[b]

HOUSES

A large number of prehistoric house remains are known in the Germanic and particularly in the Scandinavian countries (*Mannus-Bibliothek*, xi, 1913). The oldest iron-age houses, datable well before the Christian era, are in the Jutland peninsula (*Fra National-museets Arbeidsmark*, 1928, 1930). The largest group, consisting of foundations of some eleven hundred houses, is represented by the *kämpagravar* ('the warriors' graves') of the island of Gotland, many of which, datable to the first five centuries of our era, have been excavated.

[a] A reconstructed house at *Lojsta* in *Gotland*, set up by J. Nihlén and Gerda Boëthius.

[b] The foundations of the same house. In the foreground is the threshold; inside are the two rows of stone bases which carried the wooden posts or columns. This house is of the third century of our era but there are several others of similar ground-plan that are older. (xi, 70.)

[*Fornvännen*, 27, 1932, p. 342]

[a]

[b]

[*a*] Ornamental pin.

[*b*] Mount of drinking horn.

[*c*] Fibula.

[*d*] Roman trulla. (xi, 67.)

[*e*] Armlet.

[*f*] Collar.

[*g*] Armlet.

[*h*]–[*k*$_2$] Fibulae.

All of bronze.

[*a*], [*d*], [*g*], [*h*] found in *Finland*; [*e*] in *Latvia*, the rest in *Esthonia*. The trulla is unique as a find in this region, Roman wares being on the whole very rarely found in these countries. The fibulae are of common Germanic types, the other objects are of types that have a distribution ranging from the south-western provinces of Finland to the banks of the Vistula. (xi, 67.)

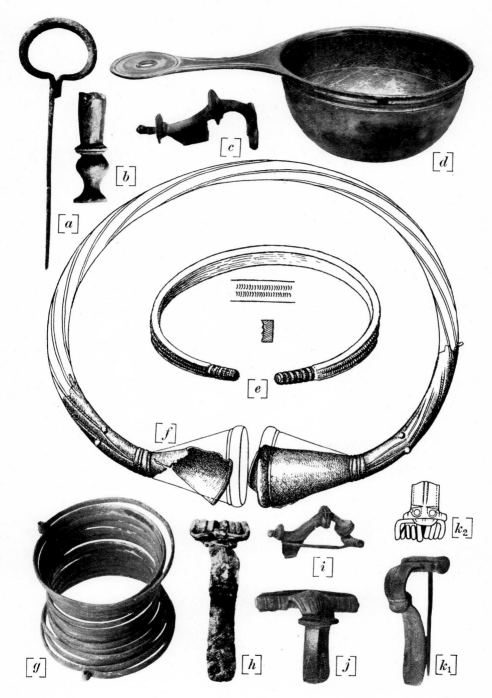

POLAND

Before the Slavs moved from their settlements on the upper Dniester south of the Pripet marshes Poland was, for the two first centuries of our era, inhabited by East-Germanic peoples, Burgundians, Vandals, etc. A trade-route followed the Vistula leading towards the south-eastern provinces of the Empire. Evidence of the extent of trade is afforded by the fact that some 20,000 Roman denarii have been found in Poland. (xi, 70, 72.)

[a], [m] Pottery bowls.

[b], [d], [j] Bronze fibulae.

[c] Gold pendant.

[e] Spearhead.

[f] Dagger.

[g] Gallo-Roman pottery kantharos with black glaze.

[h] Shears.

[i] Spindle made of amber beads threaded on a bronze wire.

[k] Bronze buckle.

[l] Iron Spur.

[a] from *Gronówko*; [b] from *Rogoźno*; [c] from *Gniew*; [d] from *Niezychowo*; [e, f, h] from *Pyszaca*; [g] from *Topolno*; [i] from *Kowanówko*; [j] from *Kokorzyn*; [k] from *Oborniki*; [l] from *Borek Fatecki*; [m] from *Kopki*.

[*Photographs supplied by Prof. J. Kostrzewski of the University of Poznań*]

[a]

[b]

[c]

[d]

[e]

[f]

[g]

[h]

[i]

[j]

[l]

[k]

[m]

[a] GOLD ANIMAL PLAQUE with ornaments of the North-Asiatic animal style found at *Mikhalkowo* (Galicia) now in the *Lwow Museum*. On the shoulder and flank are embossed circles each having a *triquetrum* design. (xi, 77.)

[b] SHAMAN CROWN in GOLD from the same find and in the same museum. The form occurs on the later Shaman crowns worn by sorcerers of northern Asia. (xi, 77.)

[c] SILVER DACIAN SPIRAL ARMLET from *Dacia* in the National Museum, *Budapest*. A Greek palmette pattern appears on the upper end. (xi, 88.)
[*Photograph National Museum, Budapest*]

[d] DACIAN POTTERY. Part of a bowl imitating Samian ware, found at *Tei*, in the National Museum, *Budapest*. (xi, 88.)
[22 *Bericht der römische-germanischen Kommission*, 1932, Pl. 20, 5]

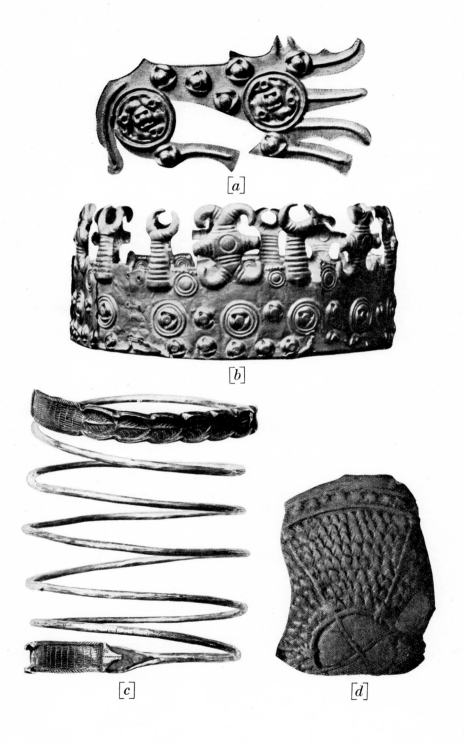

[a]

[b]

[c]

[d]

[*a*] WALL-PAINTING from a grave at *Panticapaeum*, showing a battle between Panticapaeans (to the left) and Scythian horsemen of the Crimea (to the right). (xi, 99.)

[M. Rostovtzeff, *Iranians and Greeks in South Russia*, Pl. XXIX, and *Revue des Arts Asiatiques*, 1933, Pl. LXV*a*]

[*b*] GOLD PLAQUE from *Siberia*, a Sarmatian hunting a wild boar in a forest. (xi, 100.)

[M. Rostovtzeff, *The Animal Style in South Russia and China*, 1929, Pl. XVI, 2, and *Revue des Arts Asiatiques*, 1933, Pl. LXV*b*]

[a]

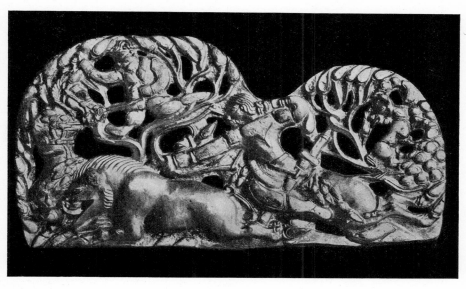

[b]

[*a*] RELIGIOUS PAINTING from *Doura*. A reconstruction by Dr F. Brown from fragments of the decoration of the Temple of Zeus Theos. (xi, 128, 637.)

[F. Brown, *Dura Report* VII–VIII, pp. 196 *sqq.* and fig. 50; cf. M. Rostovtzeff, *Dura-Europos and its Art*, 1938, Pl. XIII and p. 75]

[*b*] A PAINTED RELIEF from the Temple of Bel at *Palmyra*. (xi, 128.)

[H. Seyrig, *Syria*, XV, 1932, pp. 155 *sqq. Photograph Service d'Antiquités, Beyrouth*]

[a]

[b]

[a] A BAS-RELIEF at *Bihistun* representing the duel between Gotarzes and Meherdates. The former, in the centre, is crowned by a victory. (xi, 129.)

[E. Herzfeld, *Am Tor von Asien*, Taf. 21]

[b] PAINTING from the so-called temple of the Palmyrene gods of *Doura* in the *Damascus National Museum*. Conon and two priests performing sacrifice to the god of the temple. (xi, 129, 637, 805.)

[F. Cumont, *Fouilles de Doura-Europos*, Pl. XXXI]

[a]

[b]

[*a*] A SILVER CUP from *Sacastene* with scenes of a banquet. (xi, 130.)

[J. Smirnoff, *Argenterie Orientale*, S. Petersburg, 1909, Pl. XXXVIII, no. 67; cf. M. Rostovtzeff, "Some New Aspects of Iranian Art," *Seminarium Kondakovianum*, VI, 1933, pp. 174 *sqq.* Pl. XII, 7]

[*b*] JEWELS from *Doura*. (xi, 130.)

[*Dura Report*, IV, Pl. XXVI, cf. p. 256]

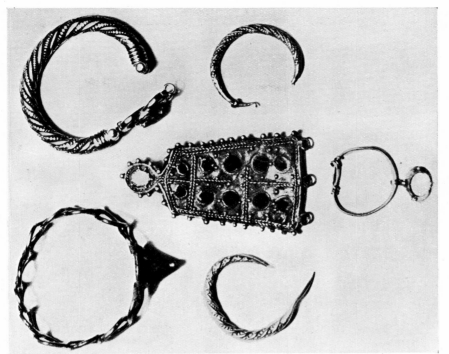

TYPES of GLAZED POTTERY from *Doura* and *Irzi* in *Mesopotamia*.

[a], [b], [d] Amphorae with moulded decoration on the shoulders. (Unpublished.)

[c] A small pot with brilliant glaze. (Unpublished.)

[e] A thymiaterion from the temple of Atargatis in *Doura*. (xi, 130.)

[M. Rostovtzeff, *Dura-Europos and its Art*, 1938, Pl. VIII, 2]
[*Photographs Yale Dura Expedition, New Haven, Conn.*]

[a]

[b]

[c]

[d]

[e]

HADRIAN'S WALL, a view of the elevated sentry-walk at House-
steads. (xi, 183, 522 *sq.*)

[*Photograph D. McLeish*]

3-2

PART of the RIBBON-LIKE RELIEF-BAND on the Column of Trajan in Trajan's Forum in *Rome*. The lower scene joins on to the upper at the right-hand side.

The army crossing the Danube by two bridges. (xi, 226, 782.) For other portions see 2, 38, 40, 84.

[C. Cichorius, *Die Reliefs der Trajanssaüle*, IV, V]

PART of the RIBBON-LIKE RELIEF-BAND on the Column of Trajan in *Rome*.

[*a*] The Roman victory at Tapae. (xi, 227.)

[*b*] Attack on a Mühlbach fortress.

On the right Romans display the heads of Dacians. (xi, 229, 782, 789.) For other portions see 2, 36, 40, 84.

[C. Cichorius, *op. cit.* XXIV and LXXII]

[a]

[b]

PART of the RIBBON-LIKE RELIEF-BAND on the Column of Trajan in *Rome*.

[*a*] Trajan setting out for the campaign in June 105.

[*b*] Trajan disembarking after his crossing of the Adriatic. (xi, 230, 782.) For other portions see 2, 36, 38, 84.

[C. Cichorius, *op. cit.* LXXXI, LXXXII]

[a]

[b]

THE GREAT MONUMENT at *Adamclisi*, dedicated to Mars Ultor in A.D. 109.

[a] View of the core.

[b] to [e] represent typical examples of the metopes which surround the monument immediately below the battlement. [b] Two Roman soldiers; [c] a mailed Roman with short sword getting the better of a Dacian in close combat; [d] a Roman soldier with two noble Dacian captives; [e] a Dacian leading his wife into exile. (xi, 234 *sq.*, 804.)

[*Photographs R. P. Longden*]

[a]

[b]

[c]

[d]

[e]

[a] TWO VOTIVE STELAE (height 1·70 and 1·85 metres) found at *Sillègue* (*Département de Constantine*), now in the *Stéphane-Gsell Museum* at *Algiers*. That on the left is dated to the year 183 of the provincial era = A.D. 222. In the upper panel is Baal-Saturn; in the central one are the dedicators, a priest and his wife, Africans of the middle class; in the lowest panel is the sacrificial animal. Local art with some attempt at realism. (xi, 488.)

[*C.I.L.* viii, 20433, 20431; P. Wuilleumier, *Musée d'Alger, Supplément*, Paris 1928, pp. 28 *sqq.*, Pl. III. *Photographs, Direction des Antiquités de l'Algérie*]

[b] STATUE in terracotta (height 1·50 m.) found near *Bir Bou Rekba* (*Tunisia*), in the ruins of a sanctuary adjoining the ancient town of *Siagu*, now in the *Bardo Museum* at *Tunis*. This lion-headed goddess personifies the *genius terrae Africae*. The statue, which stood at the entrance of a temple of Baal-Saturn and Tanit-Caelestis, is of the Roman era but perpetuates an Oriental tradition which harks back to Punic days. (xi, 488.)

[A. Merlin, 'Le Sanctuaire de Baal et de Tanit près de Siagu,' Paris 1910, Fasc. iv *des Notes et Documents publiées par la Direction des Antiquités et Arts de Tunisie*, Pl. III 1. *Photograph, Direction des Antiquités et Arts de Tunisie*]

[a]　　　　　　　　　　　　　　　　　　　[b]

SPAIN

[*a*] TWO SCULPTURES from *Castulo*, in the *Archaeological Museum* of *Madrid*: a facing bust (height 0·40 m.), with a head-dress of leaves; below a pedimental ornament flanked by volutes (height 0·42 m.) decorated with facing human heads surrounded by long pointed leaves. Native work clumsily executed. (xi, 498.)

[*Photographs by Professor Albertini*]

[*b*] A FUNERAL STELE (*Ephem. Epigr.* VIII, p. 426, no. 168), at *Luzcando* in the *Province* of *Alava* (height 1 m.): six-petalled flowers and stylized vine-tendrils are carved in low relief reminiscent of wood-carving. Below it is the fragment of a STELE (height 0·60 m.) in the collection of the Marquis of Comillas at *Comillas* in the *Province* of *Santander*. The stone is covered in designs carried out in the manner of wood-carving. (xi, 499.)

[*Photographs by F. Baraibar and Professor Albertini*]

[*c*], [*d*] POTTERY fragments found at *Elche* in the *Province* of *Alicante* now in the *Faculté des Lettres de l'Université de Bordeaux*. These fragments were found closely associated with sherds and coins of the Roman period, and are evidence for the long duration of the Iberian pottery style. The ancient type of decoration and fabric is accurately retained in the painting of the bird (height 0·16 m.); but they have experienced a certain amount of evolution in the drawing of the garland (width 0·42 m.). (xi, 499.)

[E. Albertini, "Fouilles d'Elche" in *Bulletin Hispanique*, VIII–IX (1906–07), Pl. I, 11 and Pl. VIII, 71 bis. *Photographs by La Photographie industrielle du Sud-Ouest, Bordeaux*]

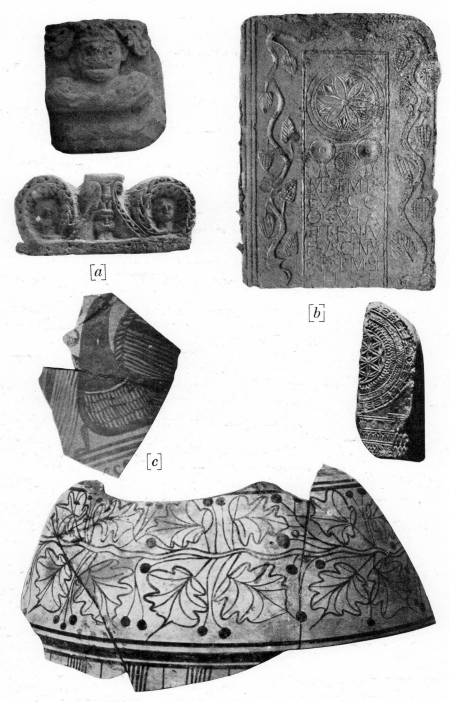

[a]

[b]

[c]

[d]

[*a*] THE ROMAN BRIDGE of *Alcantara* (*Province* of *Cáceres*) over the Tagus. Built under Trajan, the expense being shared by eleven citizens of Lusitania, it is a structure remarkable for its bold design. The length is 194 metres, the height, without the arch that rises in the middle of the bridge, is 48 metres. (xi, 500.)

[*C.I.L.* II, pp. 89–96; Dessau, *Insc. Lat. Select.* 287; J. R. Mélida, *Arqueologia Española*, p. 266 *sq.*, Pl. XIX; R. Menéndez Pidal, *Historia de España*, II, pp. 577 *sqq. Photograph* K. Hielscher, *Das Unbekannte Spanien*, Pl. 142]

[*b*] THE AQUEDUCT of *Segovia*. This aqueduct, which probably dates from the early days of the Empire, crosses a valley in the middle of the city. It bends at an obtuse angle and has arcades in two storeys. The maximum height is 28·50 metres. There was once an inscription in letters of bronze, now lost. (xi, 500.)

[J. R. Mélida, *op. cit.* p. 269, Pl. XX; R. Menéndez Pidal, *op. cit.* II, p. 297 *sq. Photograph Vernacci*]

[a]

[b]

[*a*] A GOLD BROOCH (known as the Aesica Brooch) from a Roman fort in *Northumberland*, now in the *Black Gate Museum, Newcastle-on-Tyne*. Length 11·4 centimetres.

[*b*] A CASTOR POTTERY VASE from *Corbridge* at *Corbridge*.
A dog pursuing a hare.
This pottery was made at and near *Castor* (Northamptonshire).
Both show a blend of Roman and Celtic influences (xi, 517), the shape being Roman and the ornament typically Celtic.

[*c*] THE ROMAN BATHS at *Bath*; the vaulted hall of the Great Bath. (xi, 522.)

[R. G. Collingwood, *Roman Britain*, Figs. 15, 34, 37]

[a]

[b]

[c]

4-2

[a] PAINTED POTTERY of the Vangiones from *Rheinhessen* in the *Römisch-germanisches Zentralmuseum, Mainz.* These jars closely resemble Celtic ceramics. (xi, 528.)

[G. Behrens, *Denkmäler des Wangionengebietes*, Frankfurt a. Main, 1923. *Photographs Römisch-germanisches Zentralmuseum, Mainz*]

[b] GERMAN POTTERY of the Suebi Nicretes found near *Mannheim*, now in the *Mannheim Schlossmuseum.* (xi, 528.) Scale in centimetres.

[*Altertümer unserer heidnischen Vorzeit*, v, p. 370. *Photograph Mannheim Museum*]

[c] Examples of the REVIVAL of La Tène types of pottery beginning in the later part of the second century, now in the *Landesmuseum, Bonn.* (xi, 536.) Scale in centimetres.

[F. Oelmann, *Die Keramik des Kastells Niederbieber*, Frankfurt a. Main, 1914, p. 35. *Photograph Landesmuseum, Bonn*]

[a]

[b]

[c]

[a], [b] TOMBSTONE of Blussus and his wife Menimanii from *Mainz* in the *City Museum* of *Mainz*. Both bear Celtic names and wear Celtic costume. On [b] is a detailed view of the wife with her jewelry and her small lap-dog. (xi, 534.)

[*C.I.L.* XIII, 7067. *Photographs from the painted casts in the Römisch-germanisches Zentralmuseum, Mainz*]

[c] TOMBSTONE of a Roman lady from *Nickenich*, in the Museum at *Bonn*. She wears a Celtic necklace and her hands are placed so as to display her bracelets and rings. (xi, 534.) Height 1·77 metres.

[*Germania* 16, 1932, p. 22 ff. *Photograph Landesmuseum, Bonn*]

[d] TOMBSTONE from *Neumagen* in the *Landesmuseum* at Trèves. Above, the master with horse, hound and groom return from the hunt. Below, tenants paying their dues. (xi, 534.) Scale in centimetres.

[W. von Massow, *Die Grabmäler von Neumagen*, 1932, p. 184. *Photographs Landesmuseum, Trèves*]

[a]

[b]

[c]

[d]

[a] Two views of a TOMBSTONE, in its present state above, and restored below, from the pillar of *Igel* on the Moselle, in the *Landesmuseum, Trèves*. In the central medallion Hercules ascends to heaven in a quadriga and is welcomed by Minerva. On the border are the signs of the Zodiac; in the four corners, the heads of Winds; on the side columns Mars and Venus(?) fighting against giants. (xi, 534.) Scale in centimetres.

[H. Dragendorff and E. Krüger, *Das Grabmal von Igel*, Trèves, 1924. *Photographs Landesmuseum, Trèves*]

[b] THREE DEITIES on a 'stone of the four gods' from *Alzey, Rheinhessen* at *Alzey*. Height 98·8 centimetres. At the top is Hercules with Cerberus; in the centre Vulcan with tongs and a torch, at his side is a stag; at the bottom is Juno. (xi, 538.)

[*Mainzer Zeitschrift*, 24/25, 1929–30, p. 98. *Photographs Römisch-germanisches Zentralmuseum, Mainz*]

[a]

[b]

[a] TOMBSTONE of Veriuca found at *Intercisa* (Pannonia) now in the National Museum at *Budapest*. She wears the native Pannonian dress with large fibulae (see 60 [a], [b]) on her shoulders, and holds a spindle in her right hand and a bird perched on her left forefinger. (xi, 541.)

[b] TWO FUNERAL MEDALLIONS in stone of Norican type from *Dacia* in the Transylvanian National Museum at *Cluj*. (xi, 553.)

[c] A PAIR OF STONE LIONS decorating a tomb from *Intercisa* now in the National Museum at *Budapest*. (xi, 553.)

[b]

[c]

[a]

[*a*], [*b*] THREE SILVER FIBULAE from northern *Pannonia* in the National Museum, *Budapest*. The two lower ones (from *Pátka*) are inlaid with stones and have golden filigree decoration.

[*c*] A SHERD of a grey pot by 'Resatus' in La Tène style from *Aquincum*, in the same museum.

[*d*] TWO BRONZE OPENWORK PLAQUES found in northern *Pannonia* and in the same museum used to decorate the sides of chariots. (xi, 542.)

[*Photographs National Museum, Budapest*]

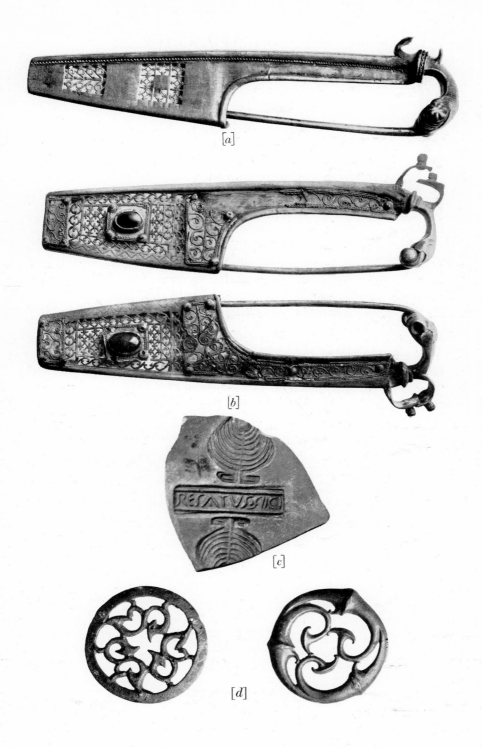

[a]

[b]

[c]

[d]

[*a*] A FUNERAL RELIEF from *Palmyra* formerly in the collection of Vicomtesse d'Andurain in *Palmyra*. A schoolboy holding tablets on which there appear the last four letters of the Greek alphabet. He wears the long-sleeved national dress and a cloak fastened by a brooch on the right shoulder, and a necklace with pendant. (xi, 639.)

[M. Rostovtzeff, *Caravan Cities*, Pl. XXIII, 3]

[*b*] A STATUE of HADRIAN from *Hierapytna, Crete* now in the *Museum of Antiquities, Constantinople*. On his breastplate there appears a relief showing the Palladium crowned by two victories and standing on the back of the She-wolf under which are the Twins. He is crowned with the imperial laurel-wreath. At his feet is a crouching boy. (xi, 666.)

[M. Schede, *Griech. und Röm. Skulpturen des Antikenmuseums, Istanbul*, Pl. XXXIII]

[a]

[b]

[*a*] THE PRAETORIUM of the camp for two legions at *Vetera* near *Xanten* on the Rhine. A model by R. Schultze. A reconstruction of the camp could be made with approximate certainty on account of the clear ground-plan revealed in the excavations. The date lies between A.D. 50 and 70, probably between 60 and 70. (xi, 776.)

[R. Schultze in H. Lehner, 'Xanten,' *Römisch-germanische Forschungen*, IV, pp. 71 *sqq.*]

[*b*] THE PALACE OF A LEGATUS at *Vetera*. A model by H. Mylius. (xi. 776.)

[H. Lehner, *ib.* pp. 52 *sqq.*; cf. G. Rodenwaldt, *Gnomon*, II, 1926, pp. 337 *sqq. Photographs Rheinisches Provinzial-Museum, Bonn*]

[a]

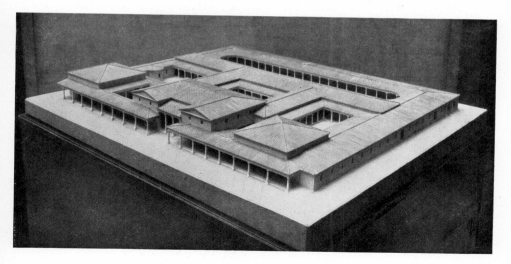

[b]

[a] THE DOMUS AUREA of Nero in *Rome*, a view of the vault of the octagonal hall in the east wing. (xi, 777.) Compare Plan 1 in Volume xi, facing p. 775.

[G. Lugli, *I monumenti antichi di Roma e suburbio*, i, 1930, pp. 200 *sqq.*; A. Terenzio, 'The Golden House of Nero', *Illustrated London News* 1934, July 21, pp. 97 *sqq.* *Photograph Illustrated London News*]

[b] WALL-PAINTING from *Pompeii* in *Naples, Museo Nazionale*. View of a building which resembles the surviving portions of the *Domus Aurea* on account of its symmetrical arrangement and central block. (xi, 777.)

[M. Rostowzew, 'Pompeianische Landschaften und römische Villen,' *J.D.A.I.* xix, 1904, pp. 103 *sqq.*, Pl. 7, 2; cf. M. Rostowzew, *Röm. Mitt.* xxvi, 1911, pp. 72 *sqq.*]

[a]

[b]

[*a*] THE EXTERIOR of the Colosseum, the *Amphitheatrum Flavium,* in *Rome.*

[*b*] THE INTERIOR. (xi, 778 *sq.*)

[See G. Lugli, *op. cit.* pp. 186 *sqq.* for the history of the structure and especially the problem of the fourth storey. Cf. H. M. Leopold, *Meded. Nederl. Histor. Inst. Rome,* IV, 1924, p. 39, and A. von Gerkan, *Röm. Mitt.* XL, 1925, pp. 11 *sqq. Photographs Alinari*]

[a]

[b]

[a] THE ARCH OF TITUS in *Rome*, set on the crest of the Velia, *in sacra via summa*, to commemorate the victory of Titus over the Jews and the capture of Jerusalem. It was only completed and dedicated after his death (A.D. 81). The original portions are of Pentelic marble, the restorations of travertine. (xi, 779.) (For the reliefs see below, 78 [a], [b].)

[G. Lugli, *op. cit.* pp. 147 *sqq.*; F. Noack, *Triumph und Triumphbogen* (Warburg Vorträge 1925–1926), pp. 183 *sqq.*; H. Kähler, *Röm. Mitt.* L, 1935, pp. 214 *sqq.*]

[b] THE ARCH OF TRAJAN at *Ancona* at the entrance of the harbour mole. Set up in A.D. 115 to commemorate the widening of the harbour. (xi, 780.)

[F. Noack, *op. cit.* p. 189. The statue-base has been studied by E. Galli, see *Arch. Anz.* 1936, p. 458, fig. 10. After F. Noack, *Baukunst*, Pl. 148]

[b]

[a]

PAINTING

[a] WALL-PAINTING: details from the House of the Vettii in *Pompeii* illustrating the fourth Pompeian style. (xi, 783 *sq.*)

[For criticism of the 'fourth style' see G. Rodenwaldt, *Arch. Anz.* 1923–4, p. 369, and *Die Kunst der Antike*³, pp. 74 *sqq.*; L. Curtius, *Die Wandmalerei Pompejis. Photograph Alinari*]

[b] WALL-PAINTING: a fragment from *Herculaneum*, in *Naples, Museo Nazionale.* (xi, 784.)

[G. Rodenwaldt, *Die Kunst der Antike*³, p. 74; L. Curtius, *op. cit.* pp. 174 *sqq. Photograph Anderson*]

[a]

[b]

PAINTING

[a] WALL-PAINTING: a wrestling-match between Pan and Eros before Dionysus and Ariadne. In the *oecus* of the House of the Vettii in *Pompeii*. This is a composition in the 'fourth style' employing Greek figure-subjects. (xi, 785.)

[G. Rodenwaldt, *Die Komposition der pompeijanischen Wandgemälde*, pp. 156 *sqq.* After Herrmann-Bruckmann, *Denkmäler der Malerei*, Pl. 9]

[b] WALL-PAINTING: Odysseus and Penelope. A painting in the 'fourth style' in the *Macellum* in *Pompeii*. It is a copy of a Greek picture to which a Roman background has been added. (xi, 785.)

[G. Rodenwaldt, *Die Kunst der Antike*³, p. 75; L. Curtius, *op. cit.* pp. 232 *sqq. Photograph Brogi*]

74

[a]

[b]

PAINTING

[a]–[c] SMALL WALL-PAINTINGS in Room *q* of the House of the Vettii in *Pompeii*. [a] Cupids busy with the vintage. [b] A cupid riding a crab. [c] A cupid driving a chariot drawn by a pair of dolphins. (xi, 785.)

[G. Rodenwaldt, *op. cit.* pp.75, 586, 588, 589; L. Curtius, *op. cit.* pp. 142 *sqq.*; Herrmann-Bruckmann, *Denkmäler der Malerei*, Pls. 25, 37. *Photographs Alinari*]

[d] DETAIL of the decoration in Room *p* of the House of the Vettii in *Pompeii*. Sea-horses. A panther balanced on a tendril. (xi, 785.)

[L. Curtius, *op. cit.* p. 29, fig. 20. *Photograph Faraglia*]

[a]

[b]

[c]

[d]

RELIEFS

RELIEFS on the inside of the Arch of Titus in *Rome* (see 70 [*a*]). Two scenes from the Triumph of Titus celebrating his Jewish victory and the capture of Jerusalem.

[*a*] Part of the procession carrying the sacred furniture captured in the Temple.

[*b*] Titus crowned by Victory in his chariot led by Virtus (on the left) and Honos. (xi, 787.)

[E. Strong, *La Scultura Romana*, pp. 105 *sqq.*, and *Art in Ancient Rome*, ii, pp. 53 *sqq.*; J. Sieveking, *Festschrift Paul Arndt*, p. 27 *sq.* *Photographs Alinari*]

[a]

[b]

[*a*] PORTION OF A FRIEZE representing Trajan in battle, cut and re-used to decorate the interior of the Arch of Constantine in *Rome*. Barbarians are shown breaking under the onslaught of the emperor and his bodyguard. (xi, 788.)

[E. Strong, *La Scultura Romana*, pp. 142 *sqq.*; J. Sieveking, *op. cit.* p. 28. *Photograph Alinari*]

[*b*] A RELIEF from one of the screens of the Rostra in the *Forum Romanum*. Trajan, addressing the people from the Rostra, proclaims the founding of *alimenta*. (xi, 788.)

[E. Strong, *op. cit.* pp. 138 *sqq.* and fig. 86*a*; J. Sieveking, *op. cit.* p. 28; E. Strong, *Art in Ancient Rome*, ii, p. 71 *sq.*; M. Rostovtzeff, *Social and Economic History of the Roman Empire*, p. 314, Pl. L, 1]

[a]

[b]

RELIEFS

RELIEFS from the Triumphal Arch of Trajan in *Beneventum*.

[*a*] The lower panel on the right pylon of the arch facing the city. Trajan is shown entering the Forum. (xi, 788.)

[*Photograph Alinari*]

[*b*] The left-hand relief on the *attica* on the side facing the city. The Capitoline Triad is shown awaiting the emperor's arrival. (xi, 789.)

[A. von Domaszewski, *Jahresh.* II, 1889, p. 137 *sq.*; E. Strong, *La Scultura Romana*, pp. 191 *sqq.* and fig. 1101; G. A. S. Snijder in *J.D.A.I.* XLI, 1926, pp. 94 *sqq.*; E. Strong, *Art in Ancient Rome*, II, p. 81]

[a]

[b]

6-2

RELIEFS

PART OF THE RIBBON-LIKE RELIEF-BAND on the Column of Trajan in Trajan's Forum in *Rome*. The lower picture joins on to the upper at the right-hand side. The scene shows the subjugation of the Dacians at the end of the First Campaign. At the left (above) is Trajan seated; on the right (below) is Decebalus standing. (xi, 782, 789.) For other portions of the same Relief-band see 2, 36–40 (above).

[E. Strong, *La Scultura Romana*, pp. 153 *sqq.*; K. Lehmann-Hartleben, *Die Traianssäule*, p. 56, Taf. 35. This after C. Cichorius, *Die Reliefs der Trajanssäule*, LXXV]

PORTRAITURE

[a] PORTRAIT of Domitius Corbulo, in *Rome, Capitoline Museum* (Stanza dei filosofi).

[H. Stuart Jones, *Catal. of the Ancient Sculpture of the Capitoline Museum*, no. 48. *Photograph Anderson*]

[b] PORTRAIT of Nero, in *Rome, Museo delle Terme*.

[R. Paribeni, *Le Terme di Diocleziano e il Museo Nazionale Romano*², no. 681. *Photograph Alinari*]

[c] PORTRAIT of a young woman of the Flavian or Trajanic period, in *Rome, Capitoline Museum* (Stanza degli imperatori).

[H. Stuart Jones, *op. cit.* no. 23; R. Delbrueck, *Antike Porträts*, Pl. 40]

[d] PORTRAIT of an elderly woman, in *Rome, Lateran Museum*. (xi, 790.)

[*Photograph Alinari*]

[a]

[b]

[c]

[d]

[*a*] STATUE of CLAUDIUS as Juppiter in *Olympia*.

[G. Rodenwaldt, *Gnomon*, II, 1926, p. 341 *sq.*; G. Lippold, *Die Skulpturen des Vaticanischen Museums*, III, 1, p. 138 *sq.*]

[*b*] STATUE of TITUS in the *Vatican* (*Braccio Nuovo*).

[W. Amelung, *Die Skulpturen des Vaticanischen Museums*, I, p. 40 *sq.*, no. 26]

[*c*] STATUE of DOMITIAN in the *Vatican* (*Braccio Nuovo*), the head separately attached but probably belonging to the statue. (xi, 790.)

[W. Amelung, *op. cit.* pp. 152 *sqq.*, no. 129. *Photographs* [*a*] *Alinari*, [*b*, *c*] *Anderson*]

[c]

[b]

[a]

[a] and [c] STATUE of the Antinous Farnese, in *Naples, Museo Nazionale*. An original of Hadrianic date based on Greek prototypes.

[G. Lippold, *Kopien und Umbildungen griechischer Statuen*, p. 192]

[b] ANTINOUS as Dionysus: head and shoulders of the Antinous Braschi in the *Vatican (Rotonda)*. A Hadrianic original. (xi, 792.)

[G. Lippold, *Die Skulpturen des Vaticanischen Museums*, III, 1, pp. 113 *sqq.*, no. 540. *Photographs* [a] *Brogi*, [b] *Anderson*]

[a]

[b]

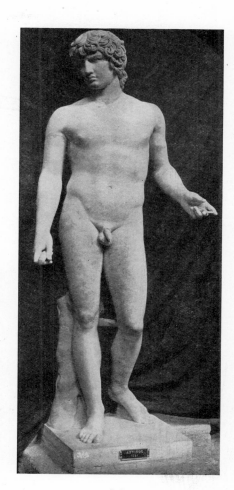

[c]

[*a*] ANTINOUS; relief in the *Villa Albani, Rome*. A Hadrianic original found in Hadrian's villa near *Tivoli*.

[G. Lippold, *Kopien und Umbildungen griechischer Statuen*, p. 192]

[*b*] ANTINOUS MONDRAGONE in *Paris, The Louvre*. Hadrianic original. (xi, 792.)

[G. Lippold, *op. cit.* p. 193 *sq. Photograph Giraudon*]

[a]

[b]

[a] STATUE of a young Centaur in *Rome, Capitoline Museum,* a work of the sculptors Aristeas and Papias of Aphrodisias in Caria made in black marble. This, with its companion piece, an old Centaur, was found in Hadrian's villa near *Tivoli.* (xi, 792.)

[G. Lippold, *op. cit.* p. 104; H. Stuart Jones, *op. cit.* no. 2. *Photograph Anderson*]

[b] STATUE in porphyry of a Dacian captive in the *Giardino Boboli* in *Florence.* The figure perhaps comes from the *porticus porphyretica* of Trajan's Forum in *Rome.* (xi, 792.)

[R. Delbrueck, *Antike Porphyrwerke,* Pl. 4a, and pp. 46 *sqq.*]

[a]

[b]

HADRIANIC AND ANTONINE SCULPTURE

[*a*] COLOSSAL PORTRAIT of Hadrian in the *Vatican* (*Rotonda*).

[G. Lippold, *Die Skulpturen des Vaticanischen Museums*, III, 1, p. 543 *sq.* no. 543]

[*b*] PORTRAIT of an unknown man, misnamed 'Vitellius,' in the *Regio Museo Archeologico* in *Venice*.

[C. Anti, *Guida del R. Museo Arch. nel Palazzo Reale di Venezia*, pp. 134 *sqq.*, no. 15; J. Sieveking, *Festschrift Habich*, pp. 43 *sqq. Photograph Fiorentini, Venice*]

[*c*] BUST in armour of Marcus Aurelius in *Rome, Capitoline Museum*; found in the so-called villa of Antoninus Pius in *Lanuvium*.

[H. Stuart Jones, *op. cit.* no. 63. *Photograph Anderson*]

[*d*] BUST in armour of Lucius Verus in *Rome, Capitoline Museum*; found with [*c*]. (xi, 793.)

[H. Stuart Jones, *op. cit.* no. 41. *Photograph Anderson*]

[a]

[b]

[c]

[d]

SARCOPHAGI

[a] PANEL of a garland-sarcophagus in the *Campo Santo* at *Pisa*. It bears the name of C. Bellicus Natalis Tebanianus, consul in A.D. 87.

[H. Dütschke, *Die antiken Bildwerke im Campo Santo zu Pisa*, pp. 101 *sqq.*, no. 128; *C.I.L.* xi, no. 1430; compare the accurate discussion of the date in W. Altmann, *Architektur und Ornamentik der antiken Sarkophage*, p. 100; J. Toynbee, *J.R.S.* xvii, 1927, p. 19 and *The Hadrianic School*, p. 229 *sq. Photograph from the Corpus of Ancient Sarcophagi*]

[b] SARCOPHAGUS with the story of Orestes, in *Rome, Lateran Museum*. The killing of Clytemnestra and Aegisthus. This was found, with [c] and a garland-sarcophagus, in a tomb of Hadrianic date near the *Porta Viminalis, Rome*.

[C. Robert, *Die antiken Sarkophag-Reliefs*, ii, no. 155; G. Rodenwaldt, *Die Kunst der Antike*³, p. 639 and *J.D.A.I.* xlv, 1930, p. 146; J. Toynbee, *The Hadrianic School*, pp. 164 *sqq. Photograph Alinari*]

[c] SARCOPHAGUS with the death of the Niobids, in *Rome, Lateran Museum*. This is the companion piece to [b]. (xi, 794.)

[C. Robert, *op. cit.* ii, no. 315; G. Rodenwaldt, *op. cit.* p. 638; J. Toynbee, *op. cit.* pp. 184 *sqq. Photograph Anderson*]

[a]

[b]

[c]

7-2

[*a*] PANEL of a sarcophagus with the Judgment of Paris, walled into the Casino of the *Villa Medici* in *Rome*. (xi, 794.)

[C. Robert, *op. cit.* II, no. 11; J. Sieveking, *Festschrift Paul Arndt*, p. 33 *sq.*, fig. 8. *Photograph Anderson*]

[*b*] THE FRONT PANEL of a large Sarcophagus, or a relief from a Triumphal arch, showing a battle in front of a fortified town; on the right and left are captives under trophies. Walled into the garden façade of the Casino of the *Villa Doria-Pamphili* in *Rome*. (xi, 795.)

[F. Matz and F. von Duhn, *Antike Bildwerke in Rom*, II, p. 433 *sq.*, no. 3319; G. Rodenwaldt, 'Über den Stilwandel in der antoninischen Kunst,' *Abh. der Preuss. Akad. der Wiss.* 1935, p. 24, Taf. 8. *Photograph from the Corpus of Ancient Sarcophagi*]

[a]

[b]

RELIEFS

TWO RONDOS of Hadrianic date attached to the Arch of Constantine in *Rome*. (xi, 795.)

[*a*] A sacrifice to Apollo.

[*b*] A sacrifice to Diana.

[E. Strong, *La Scultura Romana*, pp. 217 *sqq*. For the most recent dating see Fr. von Lorentz, *Röm. Mitt.* XLVIII, 1933, p. 311. *Photographs Anderson*]

[a]

[b]

RELIEFS

[*a*] RELIEF from a Triumphal arch; Marcus Aurelius sacrificing. In the *Palazzo dei Conservatori, Rome.*

[H. Stuart Jones, *Catal. of the Ancient Sculpture of the Palazzo dei Conservatori*, pp. 22 *sqq.*, no. 4; J. Sieveking, *op. cit.* p. 34; G. Rodenwaldt, 'Über den Stilwandel in der antoninischen Kunst,' p. 18. *Photograph Anderson*]

[*b*] RELIEF from a triumphal arch re-used on the *attica* of the Arch of Constantine in *Rome*; Marcus Aurelius sacrificing. The head has been changed. (xi, 795.)

[E. Strong, *op. cit.* pp. 253 *sqq.*; J. Sieveking, *op. cit.* p. 34; G. Rodenwaldt, *op. cit.* p. 18]

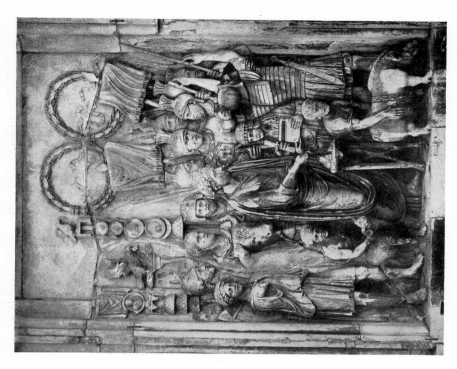

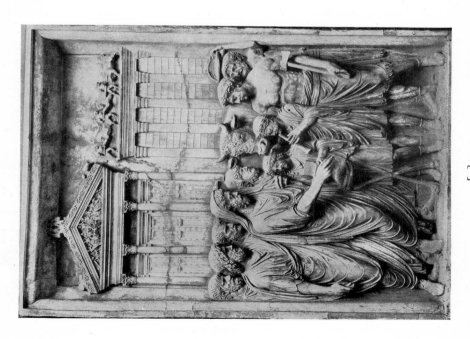

[a]

[b]

RELIEFS

DETAILS from the Column of Marcus Aurelius in *Rome*.

[*a*] In the middle of the centre band appears the miraculous storm of rain. (xi, 358, 795 *sq.*)

[E. Strong, *op. cit.* pp. 263 *sqq.*; M. Wegner, *J.D.A.I.* XLVI, 1931, p. 93, fig. 15]

[*b*] Part of Scene no. XLVIII depicting the slaughter of captive Sarmatians. (xi, 796.)

[M. Wegner, *op. cit.* p. 73, fig. 5. *Photographs German Archaeological Institute*]

[b]

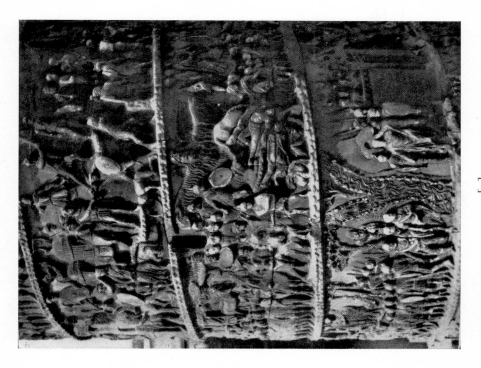

[a]

ARCHITECTURE

THE PANTHEON in Rome. (xi, 796.)

[a] The front.

[b] The interior.

[D. S. Robertson, *Handbook of Greek and Roman Architecture*, pp. 246 *sqq.*; A. von Gerkan, *Gnomon*, v, 1929, pp. 273 *sqq.*; G. Rossi, *Bull. Com.* LIX, 1931, pp. 227 *sqq.* *Photographs* [a] *Alinari,* [b] *Anderson*]

[a]

[b]

[*a*] PART OF A BLOCK of town dwellings in *Ostia*; a reconstruction. (xi, 798.)

[G. Calza, *Monumenti Antichi*, xxiii, 1915, pp. 542 *sqq.*; D. S. Robertson, *op. cit.* p. 308, fig. 129]

[*b*] LARGE TOMB with façades of red and yellow brick, the so-called 'Temple of the *deus rediculus*,' near *Rome* outside the Porta S. Sebastiano. (xi, 798.)

[*Photograph Alinari*]

[a]

[b]

[*a*] THE BATHING POOL in the great Baths of *Leptis Magna*.

[P. Romanelli, *Leptis Magna*, pp. 118 *sqq.*; D. Krencker, *Die Trierer Kaiserthermen*, pp. 216 *sqq.*]

[*b*] The Basilica of *Leptis Magna*. (xi, 798.)

[P. Romanelli, *op. cit.* p. 101 *sq.*; R. Bartoccini, *Africa Italiana*, ii, 1928–9, pp. 30 *sqq.* and p. 36. *Photographs Sopraintendenza degli Scavi, Tripolis*]

[a]

[b]

[*a*] HEAD of a bearded man in *Athens, National Museum.* (xi, 801.)

[S. Papaspyridi, *Guide du Musée National d'Athènes*, p. 114, no. 419; A. Alföldi, *Die Vorherrschaft der Pannonier im Römerreiche* (25 Jahre Röm.-German. Kommission), pp. 40 *sqq.*, where it is dated, but unconvincingly, to the third century]

[*b*] HEAD of a youth in *Berlin, Altes Museum.*

[G. Rodenwaldt, *Die Kunst der Antike*³, Taf. XLI; C. Blümel, *Römische Bildnisse*, p. 31, no. 74, Taf. 46]

[*c*] ATTIC SARCOPHAGUS, with the hunt of the Calydonian boar, in *Athens, National Museum.* (xi, 801.)

[S. Papaspyridi, *op. cit.* p. 223, no. 1186; C. Robert, *Die Antiken Sarkophag-Reliefs*, III, 2, no. 216. *Photographs* [*a*], [*c*] *German Archaeological Institute*]

[a]

[b]

[c]

[a] GARLAND-SARCOPHAGUS for a child, from southern *Asia Minor,* in the *Vatican.* (xi, 801.)

[G. Rodenwaldt, *J.H.S.* LIII, 1933, p. 198, figs. 11 and 12. *Photograph Moscioni*]

[b] FRONT of a PILLAR-SARCOPHAGUS from *Asia Minor* in *Melfi.* The coiffure of the reclining woman dates the work between A.D. 165 and 170. (xi, 801.)

[R. Delbrueck, *J.D.A.I.* XXVIII, 1913, p. 277 *sq.*; C. R. Morey, *The Sarcophagus of Claudia Antonia Sabina (Sardis,* v, 1), p. 34 *sq.*; *Antike Denkmäler,* III, Pl. 22]

[a]

[b]

[a] THE FAÇADE of the Library in *Ephesus*; a reconstruction. It was built about A.D. 115.

[W. Wilberg, *Jahresh.* xi, 1908, p. 118 *sq.*; D. S. Robertson, *op. cit.* pp. 289 *sqq.*, fig. 120]

[b] THE MONUMENTAL GATEWAY of the southern market place of *Miletus*, re-erected in the *Pergamon-Museum* in *Berlin*. (xi, 802.)

[H. Knackfuss, 'Der Südmarkt,' *Milet, Ergebnisse der Ausgrabungen,* i, 7. *Photograph Staatliche Museum, Berlin*]

[a]

[b]

RELIEF from *Wadi el Miyah* to the east of *Palmyra*, in the Museum of *Damascus*. The dedication of a Strategos to a group of gods in A.D. 225. (xi, 804.)

[H. Seyrig, *Syria*, XIII, 1932, Pl. LVI, and pp. 259 *sqq.*]

RELIEF from a tombstone from *Neumagen,* in *Trèves, Rheinisches Landesmuseum.* A School. (xi, 805.)

[*a*] Head of the teacher.

[*b*] Head of the standing pupil on the right.

[*c*] The complete scene.

[W. von Massow, *Die Grabmäler von Neumagen*, pp. 132 *sqq.*, no. 180, Taf. 27, figs. 86, 87. *Photographs Rheinisches Landesmuseum, Trèves*]

[a]

[b]

[c]

[a]–[c] Iranian types. The king on horseback on first and second-century coins of [a] *Bosporus, Sauromates II*, bronze with his bust. [b] *Parthia, Artabanus III*, tetradrachm, his bust facing. Rev. Tyche offering him a palm-branch. [c] Graeco-Sacian tetradrachm of *North-West India, Azilises*, the Dioscuri facing. (xi, 97.)

[d]–[g] *Parthia*. [d] *Vardanes*, or his son, tetradrachm A.D. 55–56. His bust. Rev. seated king and standing Tyche. [e] *Vologases I*, tetradrachm A.D. 51–52; [f] similar, A.D. 62–63; both with the same types as [d]. [g] *Osroes*, bronze *ca.* A.D. 106, head of king. Rev. Head of Tyche. (xi, 90.)

[h]–[m] Coins of *Vespasian*. [h] Denarius. His head laureate. Rev. Heads of Titus as Consul and Domitian as Praetor facing one another, both have the title Caesar. (xi, 6.) [i] Denarius. His head. Rev. Captive Judaea. [k] Sestertius. His bust. Rev. ADSERTORI LIBERTATIS PVBLICAE in wreath. [l] Similar. Rev. AETERNITAS P.R. Victory greeting the Emperor. [m] Similar. LIBERTAS RESTI-TVTA. The Emperor raising a kneeling figure while Roma stands in the background. (xi, 5.)

[n], [o] Coins of *Domitian*. [n] Silver piece of three denarii minted in Asia. His head. Rev. The Capitoline temple restored. A.D. 82. (xi, 34.) [o] Silver piece of five denarii. His head. Rev. Captive Germania in attitude of mourning seated on shields. A.D. 85. (xi, 24.)

[All in the *British Museum*]

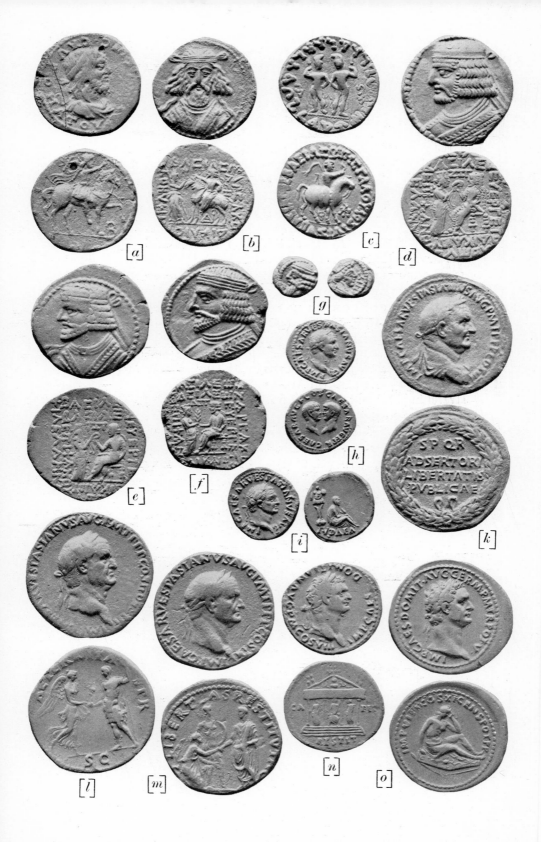

[a]

[b]

[c]

[d]

[g]

[e]

[f]

[h]

[i]

[k]

[l]

[m]

[n]

[o]

[a]–[e], [i] Coins of *Nerva*, all with laureate bust. [a] to [c] Sestertii, the first with figure of Libertas. (xi, 192.) [b] Palm tree and FISCI IVDAICI CALVMNIA SVBLATA. A.D. 96. (xi, 35, 191.) [c] Modius with corn, PLEBEI VRBANAE FRVMENTO CONSTITVTO. A.D. 97. [d] Aureus. CONCORDIA EXERCITVVM, clasped hands. (xi, 191.) [e] Denarius. Rev. Justice. (xi, 191.) [i] Sestertius. Mules grazing. VEHICVLATIONE ITALIAE REMISSA. (xi, 192.)

[f]–[h], [k], [l] Coins of *Trajan*, all with laureate bust. [f] Denarius. Rev. Figure of Spes. [g] Aureus. Rev. ALIM. ITAL. The Emperor stretching his hand towards kneeling figures. (xi, 211.) [h] Denarius. ARAB. ADQ. Figure of Arabia, a camel at her side. A.D. 108. (xi, 237.) [k] Sestertius. Rev. A triple triumphal arch. A.D. 100. (xi, 205.) [l] Sestertius. Rev. Bird's-eye view of the harbour of Ostia enlarged by Trajan. (xi, 208.)

[All except [k] in the *British Museum*; [k] in the *Bibliothèque Nationale, Paris*]

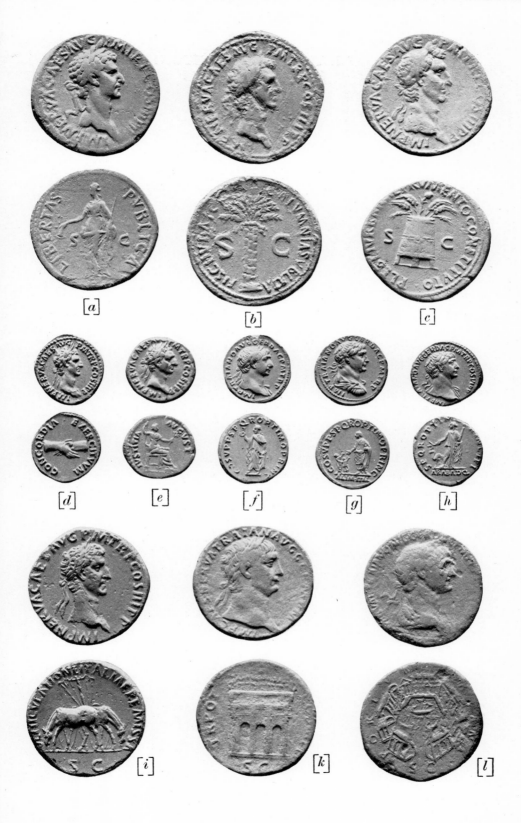

[a]

[b]

[c]

[d]

[e]

[f]

[g]

[h]

[i]

[k]

[l]

[a]–[i] Coins of *Hadrian* illustrating the types of many of the Provinces. [a] Aureus. Africa wearing an elephant-scalp. [b] Denarius. Asia, her foot on a prow. [c] Denarius. Germania armed. [d] Aureus. Hispania reclining, a voracious rabbit beside her. [e], [f] Denarii. Achaia, and Gallia, each being raised by the Emperor as *Restitutor*. [g] Dupondius. Britannia seated. [h] Denarius. Italia standing. [i] Dupondius. The device of Sicily—Triskeles with Gorgoneion. (xi, 317; xii, 415.)

[k]–[s] Coins of *Antoninus Pius*. [k] Denarius. Figure of Aequitas. (xi, 331.) [l], [m] Sestertii commemorating the giving of kings to the dependent Armenians and to the Quadi. (xi, 336.) [n] Aureus. Bust of Diva Faustina. Rev. PVELLAE FAVSTINIANAE. A two-storeyed building; above three personages in consultation, below a group of girls. (xi, 335.) [o] Aureus. The Emperor on a platform supervising a distribution of gifts. [p] Denarius. Minerva holding a Victory. [q] Sestertius. The front of the Temple of Roma begun by Hadrian and completed by Pius. (xi, 338.) [r] Bronze minted in *Alexandria* A.D. 145. Rev. In the centre head of Sarapis, around this a zone of heads of Greek gods, outside this the signs of the zodiac. (xi, 338.) [s] Similar mintage. Rev. The river-gods Nile and Tiber clasping hands. (xi, 339.)

[All in the *British Museum*]

128

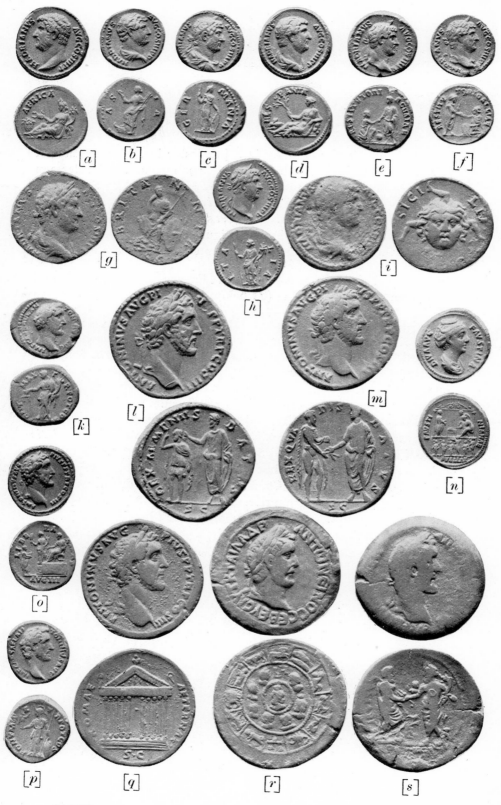

[a]   [b]   [c]   [d]   [e]   [f]

[g]   [h]   [i]

[k]   [l]   [m]   [n]

[o]   [p]   [q]   [r]   [s]

COINS OF MARCUS AURELIUS, VERUS AND
COMMODUS

[a]–[d] Coins of *Marcus Aurelius*. [a] Sestertius. Subjugation of Germany; a trophy between a seated German woman and a German captive with hands bound behind him. (xi, 357.) [b] Sestertius. RELIG AVG. Statue of the Egyptian Hermes in a temple. (xi, 357, 365; xii, 413.) [c] Sestertius. Marcus as *Restitutor Italiae*. (xi, 357.) [d] Bronze minted in *Alexandria*. Figure of MONHTA symbolizing the close link between Rome and Alexandria. (xi, 365.)

[f] *Lucius Verus*. Bronze minted in *Alexandria*. Rev. Verus and Marcus in a quadriga facing (cf. below, 212, 214).

[e], [g]–[p] Coins of *Commodus*. [e] Denarius. Romulus as conqueror. (xi, 365.) [g] Sestertius. The Emperor arriving on horseback. A.D. 180. (xi, 378.) [h] Denarius. Rev. HERCVLI ROMANO AVG. Emperor as Hercules. (xi, 387, 390; xii, 413.) [i] Denarius. Victory placing on palm-stem a shield inscribed VO . DE. commemorating the Senate's vows for the completion of the first decade of the Emperor's tribunician power. (xi, 379.) [k] Denarius. *Juppiter Exsuperantissimus* enthroned. (xi, 388; xii, 416.) [l] *Juppiter Defensor Salutis augusti* striding to left. [m] Sestertius. Janus within his temple. (xi, 388.) [n] Dupondius. The *vota decennalia* as [i]. [o] Dupondius. HERC.ROM.CONDITORI. Commodus as Hercules driving a plough with oxen in the foundation rite. (xi, 390; xii, 413.) [p] Sestertius. Commodus grasping the hand of Sarapis beside whom is Isis, an altar between them; Victory crowns the Emperor. (xi, 390; xii, 415.)

[[e], [o] in the *Bibliothèque Nationale, Paris*; the rest are in the *British Museum*]

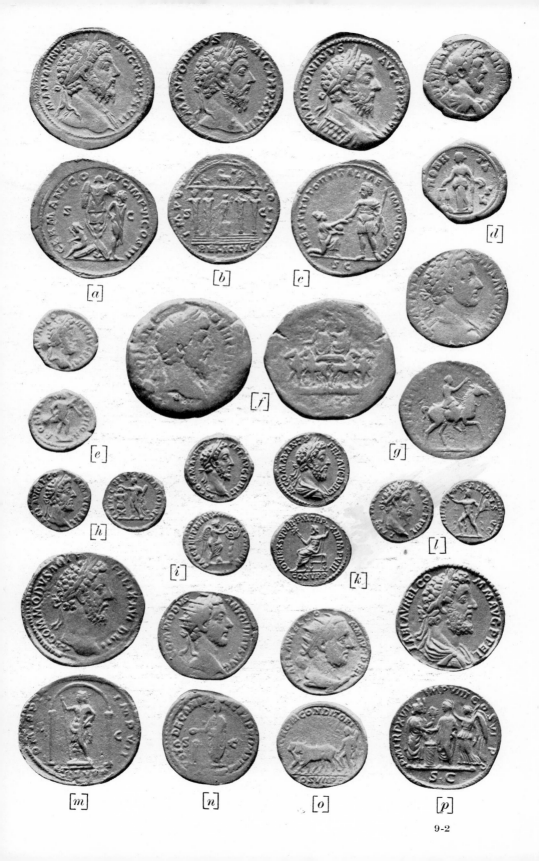

[*a*]–[*c*] A bas-relief and two figures of bodhisattvas carved in stucco found at *Rawak* near *Khotan*. There is strong Hellenic influence both in the proportions and in the treatment of the drapery. First century of our era. (xii, 98.)

[*d*] Impression of a sealing, of the same period and from the same site, Athena holding thunderbolt and aegis. For an earlier version of the type cf. a coin of Antigonus Gonatas, Volume of Plates iii, 2, *g*. (xii, 98.)

[M. A. Stein, *Ancient Khotan*, ii, Pls. XV*a*, LXXXVI, and title page vignette]

[a]

[b] [c] [d]

[*a*] An ornamental plate for harness or armour cast in bronze, from *China*, but of *Siberian* manufacture, in the *Stoclet Collection, Brussels.* A combat between a tiger and a horse; cf. the tiger 138*c*.

[*b*] An ornamental plate from a girdle clasp, cast in gold once ornamented with coloured inlays, from *Siberia*, in *Leningrad.* A horned and winged 'Persian' lion-griffin attacking a horse. For the lion-griffin, cf. Volume of Plates iii, 90, *f.* (xii, 100.)

[G. Borovka, *Scythian Art*, Pls. 47, 46*a*; E. H. Minns, *Scythians and Greeks*, p. 276, fig. 198]

[*c*] B R O N Z E K N I F E of the type that is found both at Minusinsk and on the borders of China round the bends of the Huang-ho. (xii, 101.) This specimen from *Minusinsk* is in the *Musée Cernuschi, Paris.*

[*Photograph Musée Guimet, Paris*]

[a]

[b]

[c]

[a] GOLD DIADEM found at *Novocherkask* on the lower Don, in the *Hermitage, Leningrad*. Third century of our era. In the centre (left-hand side of the figure) is a female bust carved in chalcedony; pearls, garnets, and amethysts are inset; on the upper rim are *cervidae*, trees, and water-fowl. (xii, **100**.)

[E. H. Minns, *op. cit.* p. 233, fig. 138; M. Ebert, *Reallexikon der Vorgeschichte*, IX, p. 129 *sq.* Pl. 175]

[b] A SWORD, and a large SPIRAL TORQUE of gold (detail of its end above), both from *Prochorovka* in the province of *Orenburg*, now in *Leningrad*. (xii, **101**.) These objects are closely related to the products of Sarmatian art.

[M. Ebert, *op. cit.* X, p. 317 *sq.* Pls. 112B, 112A]

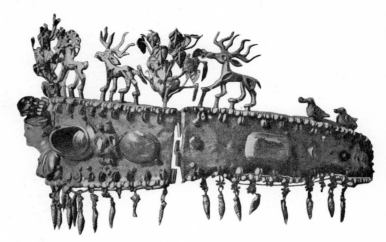

[a]

[b]

[a] A FOAL, [b] A DOE, [c] A TIGRESS suckling a fawn, all in bronze, from *Ordos*. Examples of the animal style all in the *Musée Cernuschi, Paris*. (xii, 101.)

[d] A group of smaller objects in the same museum. The two knives are from *Minusinsk*, while the clasps and buckles in animal style are from *Ordos*. (xii, 101.)

[*Photographs Musée Guimet, Paris*]

138

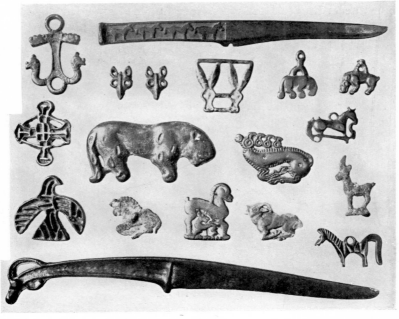

[d]

SASSANID PERSIA

[*a*] Ruins of a FIRE-TEMPLE at *Shapur* excavated in 1935–36. In the foreground is seen the external vaulted corridor leading to the main building. (xii, 120.)

[G. Salles and R. Ghirshman, *Revue des Arts Asiatiques*, x, 1936, Pl. XL]

[*b*] Remains of the PALACE at *Ctesiphon*, now called *Taq-e-Kesra*, built, according to Herzfeld's view, under Shapur I. (xii, 122.)

[a]

[b]

[*a*] Relief of ARDASHIR I at *Naqsh-e-Rustam* near *Persepolis*. In the larger relief the king is on the left and facing him is Ormuzd, likewise on horseback, handing the king the ribboned ring, symbol of royal power.

[*b*] Relief of VAHRAM I on the rock of *Shapur* near *Kazerun*. The god on horseback on the left hands the ribboned ring to the mounted king. (xii, 123.)

[F. Sarre and E. Herzfeld, *Iranische Felsreliefs*, Pls. 5, 41]

[a]

[b]

[*a*] MANICHAEAN MINIATURES depicting, on the left, a group of priests writing at their desks; and on the right above, musicians. (xii, 124f.)

[A. von Le Coq, *Chotscho*, Pl. 5; A. Christensen, *L'Iran sous les Sassanides*, p. 199, fig. 10]

[*b*] A monument in honour of SHAPUR I at *Shapur*, constructed by Roman workmen. On the shaft of one of the columns is a Pahlavi inscription. (xii, 125.)

[*Revue des Arts Asiatiques*, x, 1936, Pl. XLII]

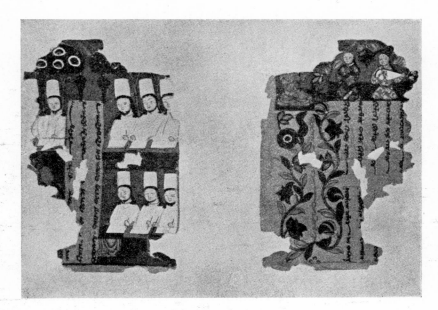

[a]

[b]

[*a*] SILVER CUP in the *British Museum* representing SHAPUR I hunting deer.

[*b*] SILVER CUP in *Leningrad* with a picture of VAHRAM I, before his accession to the throne, hunting wild boar. Dated 272/73. (xii, 125.)

[K. Erdmann, *Jahrbuch der preuss. Kunstsammlungen*, LVII, 1936, p. 197, figs. 2, 1]

[a]

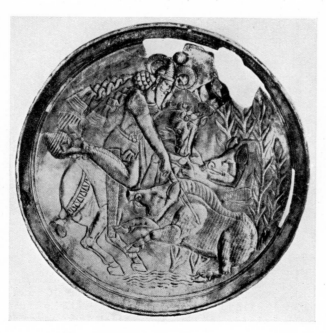

[b]

The great relief at *Naqsh-e-Rustam* near *Persepolis* (cf. Volume of Plates i, 314, *b*) with S H A P U R I on horseback receiving the submission of the captive Emperor Valerian. The standing figure in Roman garb is Kyriades. (xii, 123, 135, 559.)

[M. Dieulafoy, *L'Art antique de la Perse*, v, Pl. 15]

[*a*] Scale trapper of leather and bronze for a horse, found at *Doura*, in such good preservation that it can still be worn by a horse. Cf. the charger with scale-armour on one of the Doura graffiti, Volume of Plates iv, 26, *c*. (xii, 216.)

[*The Excavations at Dura-Europos, Preliminary report of the Sixth Season*, 1932–33, Pl. XXII, 3]

[*b*] Detail from the ARCH OF GALERIUS at *Salonica*. In the centre an *adlocutio* by the emperor; on either side of him are his bodyguards who wear the scale-armour and conical helmets of Iranian cataphracts. Their standards are Iranian *dracones*. (xii, 216, 218, 566.)

[*Photograph German Archaeological Institute*]

[a]

[b]

COMMERCE

[*a*] Handle of a SILVER PATERA found at *Capheaton* in *Northumberland*, now in the *British Museum*. In the centre is a female bust; on the left a traveller with pack and staff; on the right a shepherd and flock. The patera was probably made in Britain and its figures symbolize the commerce and prosperity of the land. (xii, 245.)

[M. Rostovtzeff, *J.R.S.* xiii, 1923, p. 99; and *Social and Economic History of the Roman Empire*, Pl. XXXI, 3]

[*b*] MOSAIC of *Madeina* in *Africa*, now in the *Musée Alaoui* at *Tunis*. It comes from the *frigidarium* of a bath in a mansion at *Althiburos*. There is a great variety of ships, river and sea-going, most of which are designated by their special names, some of them both in Greek and in Latin. At the top is a river-god seated among reeds; at the bottom the head of Ocean surrounded by fish. (xii, 245.)

[M. Rostovtzeff, *op. cit.* Pl. XXII. *C.I.L.* viii, 27790]

[a]

[b]

[*a*] Three beakers of pottery of CASTOR ware from the *Nene Valley*. They are examples of third to fourth-century metallic lustre-ware. The centre vase has a relief-scene of a chariot-race. (xii, 290.)

[*b*] Two beakers and a bottle of *New Forest* ware. The vase on the left has a lustrous glaze, that in the centre has stamped designs, and the one on the right painted lines. (xii, 291.)

[*Photographs British Museum*]

[a]

[b]

[*a*] PAINTING on a circular wooden panel (diameter 30·5 cm.) from *Egypt,* now in the *Antiquarium, Berlin.* Septimius Severus and Julia Domna with their two sons in front of them. The features of Geta have been purposely defaced (cf. below, **230,** *g*). The Emperor wears the *vestis alba triumphalis* and is crowned, like his son, with a golden garland set with gems. (xii, **364.**)

[*Die Antike,* xii, 1936, p. 157 *sq.* Pls. 10, 11]

[*b*] Two views of a marble pilaster-cap found in *Rome* from the temple of Elagabalus and Tanit on the Palatine. In the centre is the god's conical stone set on a stool. The eagle of Juppiter is in front of the stone. On the left Minerva lays a hand on the stone, on the right another goddess (Juno? Tanit?) places her hand upon it. To the right of this goddess is Victory sacrificing a bull. (xii, **55.**)

[A. B. Cook, *Zeus,* iii, p. 903 *sq.,* fig. 744; E. Strong, *Art in Ancient Rome,* ii, p. 148; and *Roman Sculpture from Augustus to Constantine,* pp. 307 *sqq.,* Pl. 94]

[a]

[b]

[*a*] BRONZE GROUP in the *Metropolitan Museum, New York*, representing the Great Mother enthroned on a four-wheeled cart drawn
by a pair of lions. She wears a veil over a mural crown and holds a
patera and a tympanum. (xii, 423.)

[*Photograph Metropolitan Museum, New York*]

[*b*] The end of a ROMAN ALTAR now in the *Fitzwilliam Museum,
Cambridge*. Four Galli carry an oblong bier on poles, upon this is
the throne of Cybele facing; under the throne is a footstool and upon
it a cushion supporting a shell-shaped receptacle within which is a
round wickerwork basket having a conical cover. On either side of
the throne is the statuette of a Gallus on a pedestal facing. (xii,
423.)

[E. M. W. Tillyard, *J.R.S.* vii, 1917, pp. 284 *sqq. Photograph E. M. W. Tillyard*]

[a]

[b]

[a] RELIEF from *Aricia,* now in the *Terme Museum, Rome.* A sacred dance of votaries; on a platform are onlookers clapping their hands, above various Egyptian deities in niches, below a frieze of ibises. (xii, 426.)

[b] RELIEF in the *Vatican,* a procession headed by a priestess of Isis followed by two priests and a girl who carries a sistrum and a ladle for holy water. (xii, 426.)

[F. Cumont, *Religions orientales dans le Paganisme romaine,*⁴ 1929, Pl. VIII, 2, 1]

[a]

[b]

MITHRAISM

[*a*] BRONZE COLLECTION BOX probably from *Syria* in the Cabinet de Médailles of the *Bibliothèque Nationale, Paris*. It bears an inscription for "Lady Atargatis" and the names of several donors. Its diameter is 15·5 cm. (xii, 428.)

[F. Cumont, *Aréthuse*, 1930, pp. 41 *sqq.*, Pl. VIII. *Photograph Bibliothèque Nationale, Paris*]

[*b*] RELIEF from the front of a MITHRAIC ALTAR found near *Heddernheim*, now in the *Museum* at *Wiesbaden*. Mithras slays the bull, a dog laps its blood, on his mantle is perched a crow; a snake, a crater and a lion are under the bull, on either side are torch-bearers. Above this scene are the twelve signs of the zodiac. Over this are depicted episodes of the Mithras myth and at the top Sol and Luna, while the sides of the carving have symbols of Winds and Seasons. (xii, 429.)

[A. B. Cook, *Zeus*, I, pp. 516 *sqq.*, fig. 389]

[a]

[b]

[a] TWO WALL-PAINTINGS from the Mithraeum at *S. Maria di Capua*, representing scenes in a ceremony of initiation. Above there appears a scene of simulated death; below the initiate, his hands bound behind his back, is offered a wreath on a sword. (xii, 429.)

[A. Minto, *Notizie degli Scavi*, 1924, pp. 353 *sqq.*]

[b] RELIEF on one side of a tombstone from *Andernach*, now in the Museum at *Bonn*. Under a shield of Amazonian shape is a figure of Attis in an attitude of mourning, common on many monuments of this region. (xii, 436.)

[A. B. Cook, *Zeus*, II, p. 310, fig. 199. Cf. H. Graillot, *Le Culte de Cybèle Mère des Dieux*, p. 438, Pl. XI]

[a]

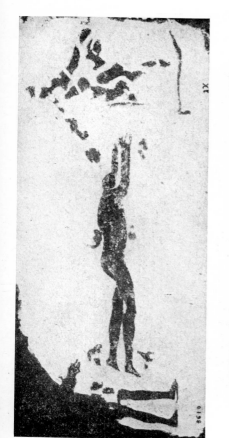

XI

[b]

A reconstructed model of the CHRISTIAN CHURCH built at *Doura* in A.D. 232. Under the decorated archway is a fresco showing the flock of the Good Shepherd. On the long wall the upper register has frescoes depicting the healing of the paralytic and Peter walking on the sea. In the lower register are the three Marys beside a sarcophagus-like tomb over which are two stars. (xii, 496.)

[*The Excavations at Dura-Europos, Preliminary report of the Fifth Season*, 1931–32, Pl. XLI]

[a] SEPTIMIUS SEVERUS, a bust in the *Museo delle Terme, Rome.* (xii, 1, 545.)

[b] CARACALLA, the portrait from a bust in *Berlin.* It shows the frowning expression and leftward turn of the head affected by Caracalla in imitation of Alexander the Great. Cf. *Epit. de Caes.* XXI, 4. (xii, 1, 47, 48, 545.)

[C. Blümel, *Katal. der Sammlung antiker Skulpturen, Römische Bildnisse,* Q. 96, Pl. 59 *sq.*]

[c], [d] ELAGABALUS, a bust in the *Capitoline Museum, Rome.* (xii, 1, 52, 545, 552.)

[H. Stuart Jones, *Catal. of the Ancient Sculptures of the Capitoline Museum,* no. 55. Photographs [a, c, d] German Archaeological Institute, [b] Berlin Museum]

[a]

[b]

[c]

[d]

SCULPTURE

[*a*] THE HERACLES FARNESE, in *Naples, Museo Nazionale.* A work signed by the copyist Glycon of Athens and made for the Baths of Caracalla in *Rome*, where it was found. The prototype will have been a statue by Lysippus representing a weary Heracles. (xii, 546.)

[*Guida Ruesch*, pp. 90 *sqq.*, no. 280]

[*b*] The so-called TORO FARNESE, in *Naples, Museo Nazionale*; found at *Rome* in the Baths of Caracalla. The punishment of Dirce by Amphion and Zethus. This marble group had a Greek painting as its prototype. (xii, 546.) See also Volume of Plates iii, 128, *b*.

[*Guida Ruesch*, pp. 80 *sqq.*, no. 260. F. Studniczka, *Zeitschrift für Bildende Kunst*, xiv, 1903, pp. 171 *sqq. Both photographs from the Archaeological Seminar, Berlin University*]

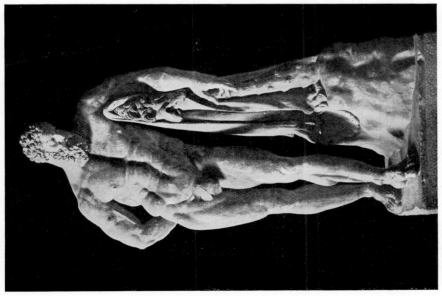

THE ARCH of Septimius Severus set up to honour him and his sons, Caracalla and Geta, in the *Roman Forum*. Dedicated A.D. 203 beside the Sacred Way by the Senate and People *ob rem publicam restitutam imperiumque populi Romani propagatum*. (xii, 10, 19, 546, 551.)

[C. Huelsen, *Il foro romano*, 1905, pp. 71 *sqq*. *C.I.L.* v, i, 1033. *Photograph Anderson*]

RELIEFS from the Arch of Septimius Severus.

[*a*] Relief above the right side archway on the face looking towards the Capitolium. A narrative scene: the Emperor addressing troops, and the siege of a city. (xii, 546.)

[E. Strong, *La Scultura Romana*, II, pp. 303 *sqq.*]

[*b*], [*c*] Reliefs on the column bases; Roman soldiers leading barbarian prisoners. (xii, 547.)

[E. Strong, *loc. cit. Photographs German Archaeological Institute*]

[a]

[b]

[c]

RELIEFS

[a] Front of a WEDDING SARCOPHAGUS in the *Villa Parisi* (formerly the Villa Taverna) in *Frascati*. The scenes illustrate the qualities of *Virtus* (Victory), *Clementia* (Mercy to conquered barbarians), *Pietas* (Sacrifice) and *Concordia* (Marriage). (xii, 547, 549.)

[G. Rodenwaldt, *Über den Stilwandel in der antoninischen Kunst*, Pl. I. *Photograph Faraglia*]

[b] Relief in the courtyard of the *Palazzo Sacchetti* in *Rome*. A seated emperor addressing the people. From some lost historical monument. (xii, 547.)

[E. Strong, *loc. cit.* pp. 306 *sqq.*, Pl. LXIII. *Photograph German Archaeological Institute*]

[c] A relief from the Tetrapylon in *Leptis Magna*. The triumphal procession of Septimius Severus and his sons. Set up *c.* A.D. 203. (xii, 547.)

[R. Bartoccini, *l'Arco quadrifronte dei Severi a Lepcis*, Africa Italiana, IV, 1931, pp. 93 *sqq.*, Fig. 73]

[a]

[b]

[c]

RELIEFS

A LION HUNT. The front of a sarcophagus in the *Palazzo Mattei* in *Rome*. (xii, 550.)

[G. Rodenwaldt, *J.D.A.I.* LI, 1936, pp. 83 *sqq*., Pl. 2. *Photograph German Archaeological Institute*]

178

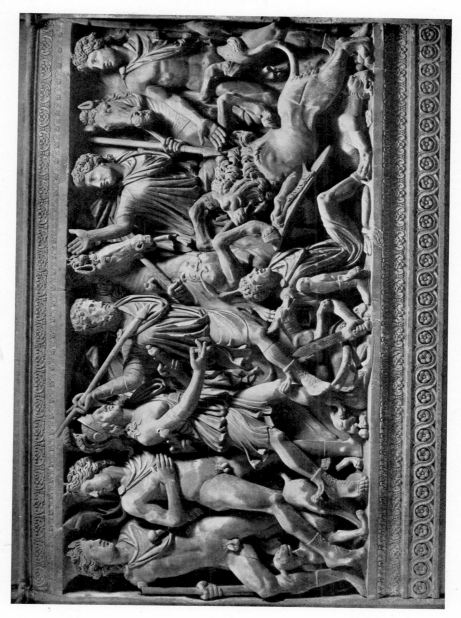

12-2

PAINTING

Paintings from the VAULT OF THE AURELII near the *Viale Manzoni* in *Rome*. (xii, 550.)

[a] The upper part of the figure of an Apostle.
[b] 'The Good Shepherd.'

[G. Bendinelli, *Mon. Ant.* xxviii, 1922–3, Pls. III, 1 and IX. G. Wilpert, *Mem. Pont. Accad. romana di Archeologia*, i, 2, 1924. F. Wirth, *Römische Wandmalerei*, 1934, pp. 177 *sqq.* (dated to *c.* A.D. 240)]

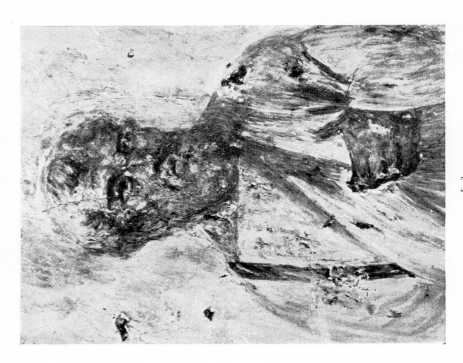

[a]

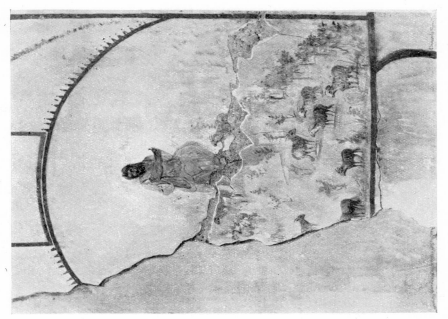

[b]

[a] Front of the PROPYLAEA of the sanctuary of the Heliopolitan Triad in *Baalbek*. A reconstruction. Built in the time of Septimius Severus and Caracalla. (xii, 551.)

[B. Schulz and H. Winnefeld, *Baalbek*, I, Pl. 41. A. von Gerkan, *Corolla Curtius*, p. 59]

[b] THE CAPITOLIUM in *Lambaesis*. Built A.D. 208. (xii, 551.)

[S. Gsell. *Les Monuments antiques de l'Algérie*, I, p. 143 *sq*. *C.I.L.* VIII, 2611]

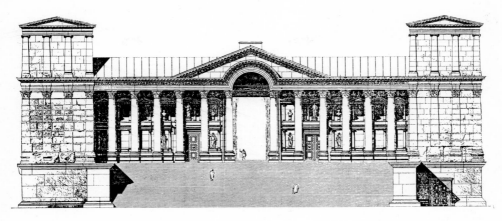

[a]

[b]

ARCHITECTURE

[a] View of the main hall of the Baths of Caracalla in *Rome*. The building was dedicated in A.D. 216. (xii, 552.)

[G. Lugli, *I Monumenti antichi di Roma e Suburbio*, I, pp. 414 *sqq*. *Photograph Alinari*]

[b] A reconstruction of the main hall of the Baths of Caracalla by G. A. Blouet.

[G. A. Blouet, *Restauration des Thermes d'Antonin Caracalla à Rome*, Paris, 1828, Pl. 15]

[b]

[a]

[a] and [b] Portrait of SEVERUS ALEXANDER in the *Vatican*. (xii, 552.)

[H. P. L'orange, *Studien zur Geschichte des spätantiken Porträts*, Oslo 1933, p. 1 *sq*. Pls. 1, 3. *Photographs German Archaeological Institute*]

[c] Portrait of GORDIANUS III in the *Berlin Museum*. (xii, 553.)

[C. Blümel, *Katalog der Sammlung antiker Skulpturen, Römische Bildnisse*, R. 102, Pl. 66. *Photograph Berlin Museum*]

[d] Portrait of DECIUS in the *Capitoline Museum, Rome*. (xii, 553.)

[H. Stuart Jones, *op. cit.*, p. 209, no. 70. H. P. L'orange, *op. cit.*, p. 43, Pl. 2. *Photograph Brogi*]

[a]

[b]

[c]

[d]

A VICTORY OVER BARBARIANS. A Roman sarcophagus for a general, from the Villa Ludovisi in the *Museo delle Terme, Rome.* (xii, 553.)

[*Antike Denkmäler*, IV, Pl. 41. *Photograph Faraglia*]

[a] A LION HUNT. A Roman sarcophagus in the *Ny Carlsberg Glyptotek* in *Copenhagen*; the so-called sarcophagus of Balbinus. (xii, 555.)

[b] Head of the central mounted hunter from the same sarcophagus.

[c] Head of a huntsman from the same.

[G. Rodenwaldt, *J.D.A.I.* LI, 1936, p. 96 *sq*. *Photographs Ny Carlsberg Glyptotek*]

[a]

[b]

[c]

[*a*] ACHILLES among the daughters of Lycomedes. Attic sarcophagus in the *Capitoline Museum, Rome.* (xii, 555.)

[H. Stuart Jones, *op. cit.* no. 1. H. P. L'orange, *op. cit.* p. 9. *Photograph Alinari*]

[*b*] HUNTING SCENE. The back of the large sarcophagus from
Sidamara in the *Museum of Antiquities, Constantinople.* (xii, 555.)

[M. Schede, *Griech. und Röm. Skulpturen des Antikenmuseum, Istanbul*, Pl. XXXIX.
C. R. Morey, *The Sarcophagus of Claudia Antonia Sabina* (Sardis, v, 1), 40]

[*c*] Sarcophagus with MUSES from the Villa Mattei in the *Museo
delle Terme* in *Rome.* (xii, 555.)

[R. Paribeni, *Le terme di Diocleziano e il Museo Nazionale Romano*, p. 76 *sq.*, no. 100.
Photograph German Archaeological Institute]

[a]

[b]

[c]

FOUR HEADS from Roman funeral monuments from *Neumagen* in the *Rheinisches Landesmuseum* in *Trèves*. (xii, 556.)

[*a*] Head of a woman from the stele of the *Negotiator*. *c.* A.D. 175.

[W. von Massow, *Die Grabmäler von Neumagen*, p. 128, Fig. 77]

[*b*] Head of the helmsman from the relief of a ship, *c.* A.D. 220.

[W. von Massow, *op. cit.* p. 208, Fig. 128]

[*c*] and [*d*] Head of a peasant from the circus monument, *c.* A.D. 220. For other sculptures from Neumagen see **122** above.

[W. von Massow, *op. cit.* p. 147, Fig. 98, p. 155, Fig. 101. G. Rodenwaldt, *Archäologischer Anzeiger*, 1927, p. 192. H. Koethe, *J.D.A.I.* L, 1935, pp. 216 *sqq. Photographs Rheinisches Landesmuseum, Trèves*]

[a]

[b]

[c]

[d]

[*a*] Portrait of GALLIENUS in the *Museo delle Terme, Rome*, in the Greek manner. (xii, 556.)

[R. Paribeni, *op. cit.* no. 736. H. P. L'orange, *op. cit.* p. 5. R. Delbrueck, *Antike Porträts*, Pl. 53]

[*b*] Portrait of GALLIENUS in the *Berlin Museum*, in the Roman manner. (xii, 556.)

[C. Blümel, *op. cit.* 114, Pl. 74. *Photograph Berlin Museum*]

RELIEFS

[*a*] SARCOPHAGUS of a pagan man and wife in the *Museo Torlonia, Rome*. The husband appears as one of the Seven Sages, the wife as one of the Nine Muses. (xii, 557.)

[G. Rodenwaldt, *J.D.A.I.* LI, 1936, p. 101 *sq.*, Pl. 5. *Photograph Faraglia*]

[*b*] SARCOPHAGUS of a Christian man and wife from the *Via Salaria* in the *Lateran Christian Museum* in *Rome*. In the centre appears 'The Good Shepherd.' (xii, 557.)

[G. Wilpert, *I Sarcofagi Cristiani*, I, Pl. I, 1. F. Gerke, *Die christlichen Sarkophage der vorkonstantinischen Zeit* (Studien zur Spätant. Kunstgesch. XI). Kap. 6, no. 10, Pl. 51, 1; Pl. 55, 1 and 2; Pl. 65, 3. *Photograph German Archaeological Institute*]

[a]

[b]

RELIEFS

SARCOPHAGUS of a philosopher (Plotinus?) in the *Lateran Museum, Rome.* (xii, 557.)

G. Rodenwaldt, *J.D.A.I.* LI, 1936, pp. 103 *sqq.*, Pl. 6. *Photograph Faraglia*]

RELIEFS

[a] WEDDING SARCOPHAGUS of an official of the *Annona* in the *Museo delle Terme* in *Rome*. (xii, 559.)

[M. Rostovtzeff, *Social and Economic History of the Roman Empire* (German ed.), I, p. 226 *sq.*, Pl. 23, 2]

[b] and [c] Heads of the man and wife on the same sarcophagus.

[G. Rodenwaldt, *Studie e Scoperte germaniche sull' Archeologia e l'Arte del tardo Impero*, Rome 1937, p. 14, Pls. II, III. *Photographs German Archaeological Institute*]

[a]

[b]

[c]

[a] PORTRAIT of a man in gold-leaf on glass inscribed *Eusebi anima dulcis,* in the *Christian Museum* of the *Vatican Library, c.* A.D. 240–250. (xii, 560.)

[C. Abbizzati, *Röm. Mitt.* xxix, 1914, pp. 240 *sqq.*]

[b] PORTRAITS of a mother with her son and daughter in gold-leaf on glass signed by the potter Bouneri in the *Museo Cristiano Civico* in *Brescia, c.* A.D. 230–240.

[C. Abbizzati, *op. cit.* pp. 274 *sqq.* F. de Mély, *Aréthuse,* iii, 1926, pp. 1 *sqq.,* Pl. II]

[a]

[b]

ARCHITECTURE

[a] THE AMPHITHEATRE in *El Djem* (*Thysdrus*) in the Roman Province of Africa. Probably built shortly after A.D. 238, since Gordianus I was there proclaimed Augustus. (xii, 76 *sq.*, 561.)

[F. Drexel, in L. Friedländer, *Darstellungen aus der Sittengeschichte Roms*, IV, p. 228 *sq.* *Photograph M. Hürlimann, Das Mittelmeer*, Zürich, 1937]

[b] THE ROUND TEMPLE in *Baalbek*. Probably built in the time of Philip the Arabian. (xii, 561.)

[D. Krencker, *Baalbek*, II, pp. 90 *sqq.*, Pl. 6]

[c] The so-called TEMPLE of Minerva Medica in *Rome*. It was perhaps part of some Baths or a Nymphaeum. (xii, 561.)

[G. T. Rivoira, *Architettura Romana*, pp. 223 *sqq.* D. Krencker, *Die Trierer Kaiserthermen*, pp. 257 *sqq.* *Photograph Alinari*]

[a]

[b]

[c]

PORTRAITS

[*a*] Portrait of PROBUS (?) in the *Capitoline Museum, Rome.* (xii, 564.)

[H. Stuart Jones, *op. cit.* no. 66, R. Delbrueck, *Bildnisse römischer Kaiser*, p. 7 *sq.*, Pl. 37]

[*b*] PORTRAIT of an unknown man in the *Landgrafenmuseum, Kassel.* (xii, 564.)

[M. Bieber, *Antike Skulpturen und Bronzen in Cassel*, pp. 34 *sqq.*, Pl. 31 and Fig. 6. G. von Kaschnitz-Weinberg, *Die Antike*, II, 1926, Pl. 7. *Photograph Kassel Museum*]

[*c*] Portrait of DIOCLETIAN in the *Villa Doria-Pamphili, Rome.* (xii, 564.)

[H. P. L'orange, *Röm. Mitt.* XLIV, 1929, pp. 180 *sqq.*, Pl. 41]

[*d*] BUST IN PORPHYRY in the *Cairo Museum.* The portrait of some member of the Imperial House, perhaps Licinius. (xii, 564.)

[R. Delbrueck, *Antike Porphyrwerke*, p. 92, Pl. 38 *sq.*]

[a]

[b]

[c]

[d]

PORTRAIT OF THE EMPEROR CONSTANTINE. Head of a colossal statue in the *Palazzo dei Conservatori, Rome.* (xii, 564.)

[R. Delbrueck, *Spätantike Kaiserporträts*, pp. 121 *sqq.*, Pl. 37. *Photograph German Archaeological Institute*]

14-2

[*a*], [*b*] BRONZE MEDALLIONS of *Alexander Severus*. On both reverses the Emperor appears as *triumphator*; on [*a*] the quadriga is in profile as on earlier representations, on [*b*] it is frontal. (xii, 558.)

[*c*], [*d*] GOLD MEDALLIONS of *Diocletian* and *Maximian* together, and of *Constantius Caesar*, son of *Constantine*. On the reverses of both are a pair of Emperors as *triumphatores* in cars drawn by teams of elephants, and the designs are frontal. (xii, 563.)

[*e*] BRONZE MEDALLION of *Probus*. His bust to left with helmet, shield and spear. Rev. an *adlocutio* by the Emperor on a platform; the scene frontally composed. Suppliant captives are in the foreground. (xii, 558.)

[[*c*] in the *Münzkabinett, Berlin*; the rest in the *Bibliothèque Nationale, Paris*]

[a]

[b]

[c]

[d]

[e]

[a] BRONZE MEDALLIC SESTERTIUS of *Postumus*. Rev. a frontally composed scene of an *adlocutio* with the Emperor and two officers on a platform. (xii, 558; and cf. 212 [e].)

[b] SILVER MEDALLION of *Alexander Severus* (cf. 212 [a], [b]). Rev. the three *Monetae*, the middle one frontal. (xii, 558.)

[c] AUREUS of *Postumus*, his head almost facing. Rev. HERCVLI THRACIO, Hercules with one of the horses of Diomede. (xii, 556, 558.)

[d] AUREUS of *Licinius*. His bust facing. Rev. Juppiter Conservator enthroned facing. (xii, 558.)

[e] GOLD MEDALLION of *Diocletian*. Rev. as last but in profile. (xii, 563.)

[f] GOLD MEDALLION of *Constantine*. His half-figure in the imperial mantle; his hands hold sceptre and globe. (xii, 563.)

[[b], [d], [f] in the *British Museum*; the others in the *Bibliothèque Nationale, Paris*]

[a]

[b]

[c]   [d]

[e]

[f]

SARCOPHAGI of the period of the Tetrarchy.

[*a*] The fall of Phaethon. Sarcophagus in the Giardino del Lago of the *Villa Borghese, Rome.* (xii, 565.)

[C. Robert, *Die antiken Sarkophagreliefs*, III, 3, Pl. 110, no. 338. G. A. S. Snijder, *Mnemosyne*, LV, 1927, pp. 401 *sqq. Photograph German Archaeological Institute*]

[*b*] A scene representing 'The Good Shepherd' and a woman praying. A Christian sarcophagus in the *Lateran Christian Museum, Rome.* (xii, 565.)

[G. Wilpert, *op. cit.* I, Pl. LVIII. *Photograph Alinari*]

[*c*] At the money-changer's or rent-collector's (?). Fragment of the lid of a sarcophagus in *Ostia.* (xii, 565.)

[*Photograph J. Rodenwaldt*]

[*d*] Christian sarcophagus with scenes from the lives of Christ and St Peter in the *Lateran Christian Museum*, no. 161. (xii, 565.)

[G. Wilpert, *op. cit.* I, Pl. CXXVII. F. Gerke, *Riv. di Arch. crist.* X, 1933, pp. 307 *sqq.* and in *Zeitschrift für Kirchengeschichte*, LIV, 1935, pp. 18 *sqq. Photograph Alinari*]

[a]

[b]

[c]

[d]

THE ARCH of Constantine in *Rome*. (xii, 547, 566, 567.)
[*Photograph from the Archaeological Seminar, Berlin University*]

CONSTANTINE

CONTEMPORARY RELIEFS on the Arch of Constantine. (xii, 566.)
[a] The battle at the Milvian Bridge.

[b] Part of the relief [a].

[c] An *adlocutio* of the Emperor to the People in the Roman Forum.

[d] Part of the relief [c].

[H. P. L'orange, *Der spätantike Bildschmuck des Konstantinsbogens* (Studien zur spätantiken Kunstgeschichte, x). *Photographs [a, c] Anderson, [b, d] German Archaeological Institute*]

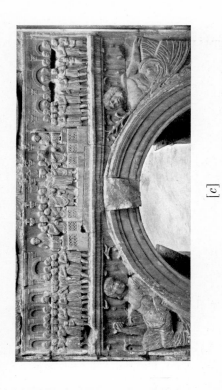

[*a*] Reconstructed M O D E L of the Imperial Baths in *Trèves*. (xii, 568.)

[Cf. D. Krencker, *op. cit.* p. 83, Fig. 92*a*]

[*b*] THE BASILICA in *Trèves*. (xii, 568.)

[H. Koethe, 'Die Trierer Basilika,' *Trierer Zeitschrift*, xii, 1937, pp. 151 *sqq.* *Photographs Rheinisches Landesmuseum, Trèves*]

[a]

[b]

ARCHITECTURE

[a] THE BASILICA of Maxentius in *Rome*. Completed by Constantine after A.D. 313. (xii, 568.)

[G. Lugli, *op. cit.* I, pp. 173 *sqq. Photograph Alinari*]

[b] A RECONSTRUCTION of the interior of the Lateran Basilica in *Rome*. (xii, 569.)

[H. Holtzinger, *Altchristliche und byzantinische Baukunst*[3], p. 39, Fig. 31. E. Josi, *Rivista di Arch. cristiana*, XI, 1934, pp. 335 *sqq.*]

[a]

[b]

[*a*] Head of a statue in armour of CONSTANTINE, in the entrance hall of the *Lateran Basilica* in *Rome*. (xii, 570.)

[R. Delbrueck, *Spätantike Kaiserporträts*, pp. 118 *sqq.*, Pl. 33 *sq.*]

[*b*] Bust in porphyry of CONSTANTINE II as Caesar (?) in the *Vatican*. (xii, 570.)

[R. Delbrueck, *op. cit.* pp. 136 *sq.*, Pl. 48 *sq.*]

[b]

[a]

RELIEF

PORPHYRY SARCOPHAGUS of Helena, in the *Vatican*. (xii, 570.)

[G. Lippold, *Die Skulpturen des vaticanischen Museums*, III, 1, pp. 195 *sqq.*, no. 589. G. Rodenwaldt, *Scritti in onore di Bartolommeo Nogara*, pp. 389 *sqq.* *Photograph Sansaini*]

15-3

[a] Aureus, bust of youthful *Caracalla*. Rev. conjoined busts of his parents, *Severus* radiate as Sol, *Domna* as Luna with crescent beneath. (xii, 35, 357.) [b] Aureus, *Geta*. Rev. Caracalla and Geta clasping hands. (xii, 36.) [c] Denarius, *Severus*. Rev. Triton reclining. (xii, 40.) [d] Denarius, *Julia Domna*. Rev. MAT. AVGG. MAT. SEN. M. PATR. (xii, 35, 52.) [e] Dupondius, *Caracalla*. Rev. Troops crossing a bridge of boats. (xii, 40.) [f] Denarius, *Elagabalus*. Rev. SANCT. DEO. SOLI. ELAGABAL. The black stone of Emesa surrounded by four parasols on a quadriga. (xii, 54.) [g] Bronze of *Stratonicea* in *Caria*. On the obverse originally busts of *Geta* and *Caracalla* facing one another, but the bust of Geta has been removed with a chisel (cf. 156 [a] above): countermarks, head of Athena and ΘEOY. Rev. Zeus Panamaros on horseback. (xii, 43.) [h] Denarius, *Severus Alexander*. Rev. FELICITAS AVG. (xii, 63.) [i] Bronze medallion, *Julia Mamaea*. Her bust as Dea Panthea with attributes of Ceres, Diana, Victoria, Abundantia and Felicitas. Rev. The Empress seated among three female figures, one frontal. (xii, 64.) [j] Denarius, *Mamaea*. Rev. FELICITAS PVBLICA. (xii, 63.) [k] Dupondius, *Severus Alexander*. Rev. RESTITVTOR MON(etae), the dupondius recoined. (xii, 65.) [l] Bronze medallion, *Severus Alexander* and *Mamaea*. Rev. The Emperor and troops crossing a pontoon bridge over the Rhine. [m] Aureus, *Uranius Antoninus*. Rev. CONSERVATOR AVG.; the black stone of Emesa on a quadriga (cf. [f]), the types to left. (xii, 70.)

[[g], [i] in the *British Museum*, [l] in *Copenhagen*, the rest in the *Bibliothèque Nationale, Paris*]

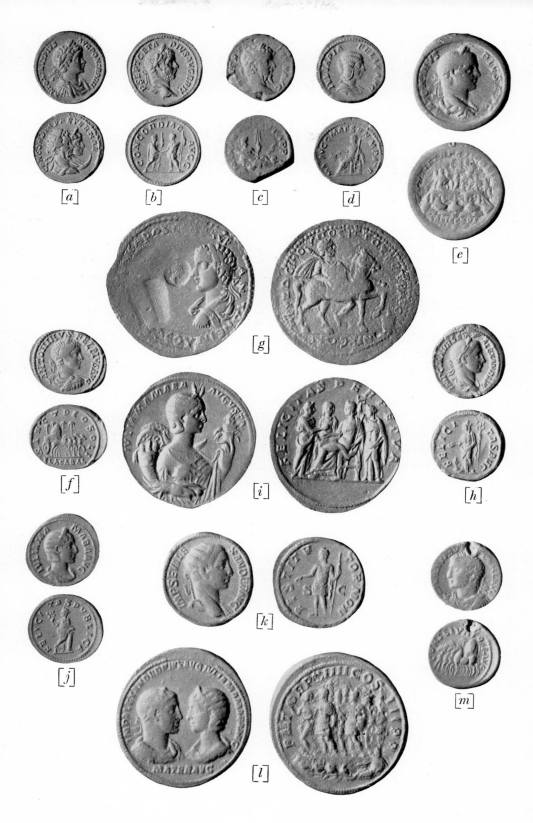

[a] [b] [c] [d] [e]

[f] [g] [h]

[i]

[j] [k] [l] [m]

COINS OF PUPIENUS, BALBINUS, MAXIMINUS, PHILIP THE ARABIAN, DECIUS, AND SOME USURPERS

[a], [c] Antoniniani of *Pupienus* and *Balbinus*. Revs. AMOR MVTVVS AVGG. and FIDES MVTVA AVGG. clasped hands. (xii, 81.) [b] Sestertius, *Maximinus*. Rev. Victory over the Germans commemorated. (xii, 74.) [d] Bronze struck at *Beroea* in *Macedon* when Philip the Arabian celebrated games there. Helmeted head of Alexander the Great. Rev. Male figure beside agonistic table. (xii, 88.) [e], [h] Antoninianus and Sestertius, both of *Philip the Arabian*, commemorating the first millennium of the foundation of the city of Rome. (xii, 91.) [f] Sestertius struck at *Philippopolis* to commemorate the consecration of *Marinus*, father of *Philip the Arabian*. Bust of Marinus over an eagle. Rev. Roma. (xii, 89.) [g] Antoninianus, *Pacatianus*. Rev. Roma and date in the year 'one thousand and one.' (xii, 92.) [i] Antoninianus, *Jotapianus*. Rev. Victory. (xii, 166.) [j], [k] Silver coins of *Regalianus* and his wife *Dryantilla*. Revs. Providentia and Pietas. They are over-struck on earlier denarii. (xii, 184.) [l], [m] Antoniniani of *Decius* and *Herennius Etruscus* commemorating a VICTORIA GERMANICA. (xii, 145.)

[[b] in the *British Museum*, the rest in the *Bibliothèque Nationale, Paris*]

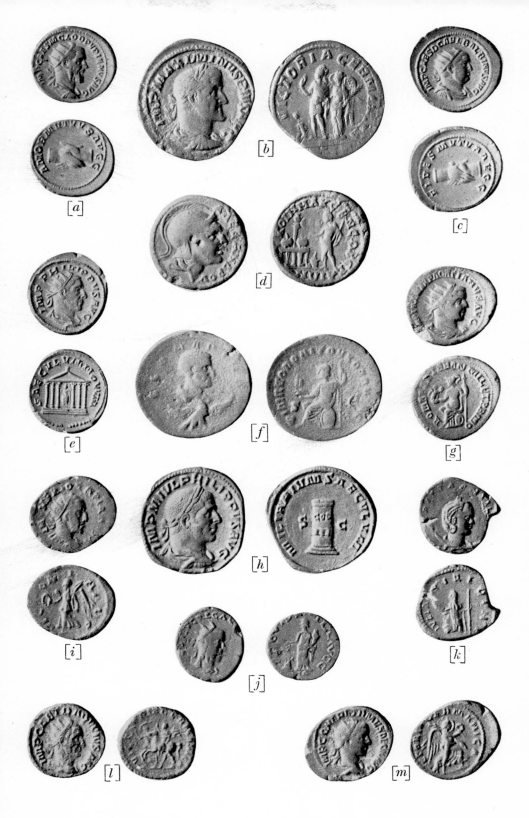

[a]

[b]

[c]

[d]

[e]

[f]

[g]

[h]

[i]

[j]

[k]

[l]

[m]

COINS OF EARLY SASSANID KINGS,
TREBONIANUS GALLUS, AND POSTUMUS

[a] to [h] Sassanid silver coins. [a], [g] *Ardashir*, his head and shoulders; on [a] there is a globe on his headdress; on [g] he wears a mural crown. (xii, 130.) Revs. A fire-altar with central column, on either side below an incense holder. (xii, 109, 120.) [b], [h] *Shapur I*, his head and shoulders; on [b] he wears a mural crown with globe; on [h] he has a helmet the crest of which ends in an eagle's head. (xii, 130.) Revs. Columnar fire-altar flanked by two attendants holding rods. (xii, 111, 120.) [c] *Vahram I*, his bust with radiate crown with globe. Rev. As [b]. (xii, 113.) [d] *Vahram II*. Jugate busts of king and queen, a small bust before them. Rev. Similar fire-altar tended by two figures. (xii, 113.) [e] *Narses*, his bust with globe-topped crown. Rev. As last. (xii, 113.) [f] *Hormizd II*; types similar to last. (xii, 114.)

[j] Dupondius of *Trebonianus Gallus*. Rev. ARN. AZI, the chief god of the Osrhoënians, Aziz, in the guise of Apollo Pythius. (xii, 199.) [i], [k] Bronze coins of *Postumus*. [i] Rev. RESTITVTOR GALLIARVM. Emperor raising kneeling figure; [k] the arms of Hercules. (xii, 187, 226.)

[i, k, in the *Bibliothèque Nationale, Paris*; the rest in the *British Museum*]

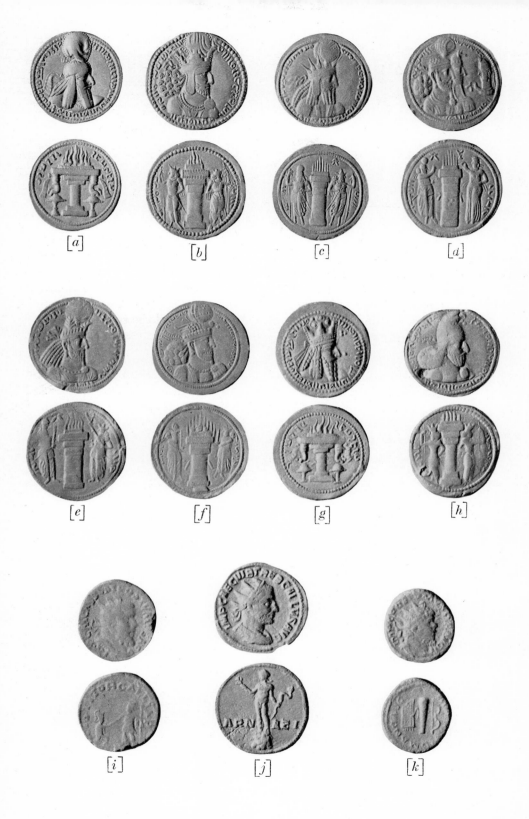

[a]

[b]

[c]

[d]

[e]

[f]

[g]

[h]

[i]

[j]

[k]

[*a*] to [*i*] A series of silver Antoniniani issued by *Decius* with heads of all the consecrated Emperors. Those represented are Augustus, Vespasian, Titus, Trajan, Hadrian, Antoninus Pius, Marcus Aurelius, Commodus, and Severus Alexander. All the reverses have the eagle of consecration. (xii, 204.)

[*j*] to [*l*] *Gallienus*. [*j*] Dupondius celebrating his return to Rome. The *Genius populi Romani* has his features. (xii, 189.) [*k*] Aureus. GALLIENAE AVGVSTAE, Gallienus in the guise of Demeter. Rev. VBIQVE PAX. Victory in chariot. (xii, 189.) [*l*] Double-Aureus in ancient gold mounting. Bust of *Gallienus*. Rev. DEO AVGVSTO, bust of Augustus. (xii, 194.)

[[*j*] in the *Bibliothèque Nationale, Paris*; [*l*] at *Parma*; the rest in the *British Museum*]

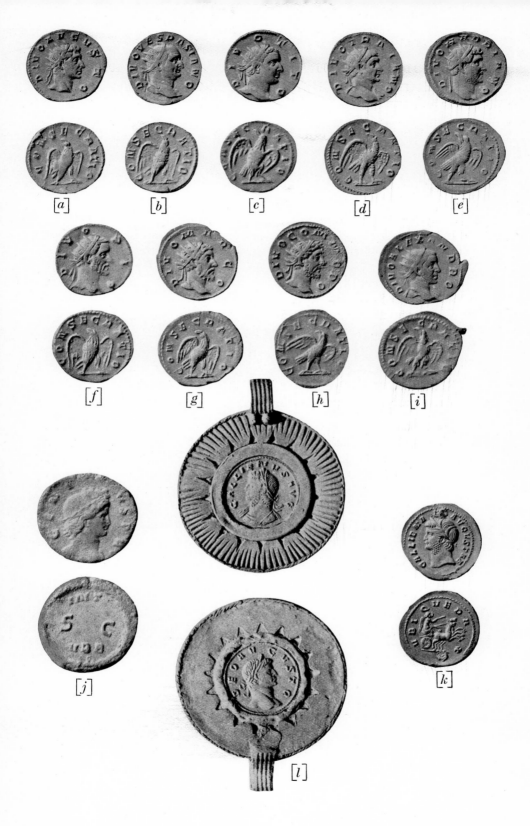

[a] [b] [c] [d] [e]

[f] [g] [h] [i]

[j]

[k]

[l]

[a] to [d] Reign of *Aurelian*, all bronze. [a] Rev. DACIA FELIX. (xii, 301.) [b] Bust of *Vaballathus* on obverse and of *Aurelian* on reverse. (xii, 301.) [c] SOL DOMINVS IMPERI ROMANI, bust of Sol. Rev. Aurelian standing sacrificing. [d] Bust of Emperor. Rev. SOLI INVICTO, Sol triumphant between captives. (xii, 309.) [e] Aureus, *Severina*. Rev. Concordia with standards. (xii, 310.) [f] Aureus, *Tacitus*. Rev. Roma. [g], [h] Bronzes, *Tacitus* and *Florian*. Revs. CLEMENTIA TEMP. (xii, 313.)

[i] to [k] *Probus*. [i] Aureus. Half-figure armed and holding a Victory. Rev. Sol the unconquered in facing chariot. (xii, 319.) [j] Bronze. Rev. Tyche of Siscia between river-gods. [k] Bronze. Rev. Hercules 'the peace-bringer.' (xii, 320.)

[l] Bronze, busts of *Carus* and Sol confronted. Rev. Felicitas. [m], [n] Aurei, *Carinus* and *Numerian*. Revs. Each Caesar as *Princeps Iuuentutis*. (xii, 324, 359.) [o] Aureus of *Postumus*, his bust conjoined with that of Hercules. Rev. Conjoined busts of Sol and Luna. [p] Aureus of *Victorinus*, his bust conjoined with that of Sol. Rev. Juppiter. (xii, 359.)

[[i], [p], in the *British Museum*; the rest in the *Bibliothèque Nationale, Paris*]

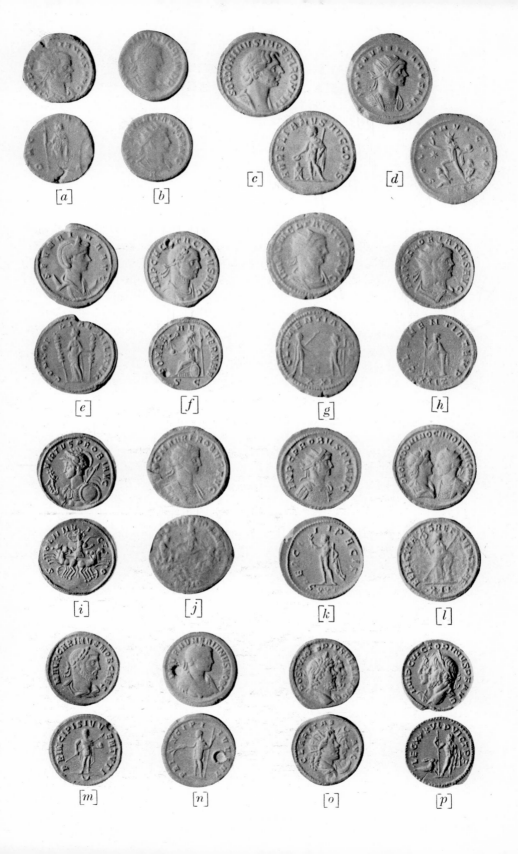

[a] [b] [c] [d]

[e] [f] [g] [h]

[i] [j] [k] [l]

[m] [n] [o] [p]

COINS OF THE TETRARCHY,
CARAUSIUS AND ALLECTUS

[a], [d] *Diocletian.* [a] Bronze. Rev. Juppiter and Hercules. (xii, 330.) [d] Aureus. Rev. The three Fates. (xii, 330.) [b], [c], [g] *Maximian*, all Aurei. [b] Hercules fighting the Hydra. [c] Rev. CONCORDIA AVGG. ET CAESS. NNNN. (xii, 330.) [g] Rev. VIRTVS ILLVRICI, the Emperor on horseback, and a war-galley below. [e], [f] *Constantius* and *Galerius* as Caesars. Rev. On each the Caesar as *Princeps Iuuentutis.* (xii, 330.)

[h], [i] *Carausius.* [h] Bronze. CARAVSIVS ET FRATRES SVI, his bust conjoined with those of Diocletian and Maximian. Rev. Pax. (xii, 331.) [i] Silver. Rev. EXPECTATE VENI, Britannia holding a trident and welcoming Carausius. (xii, 333.) [j] Bronze of *Allectus.* Rev. A war galley. (xii, 333.)

[k] Great gold medallion of *Constantius Caesar* of the weight of ten aurei (53·1 grammes). Bust of the Caesar. Rev. REDDITOR LVCIS AETERNAE. The Caesar on horseback, and a war-galley below (*cf.* [g] above). He is received by a female, personating London, kneeling in front of a city gate, beneath her LON. In the exergue PTR. From the Arras Hoard found September 1922. (xii, 333.)

[[g] to [j] in the *British Museum*, the rest in the *Bibliothèque Nationale, Paris*]

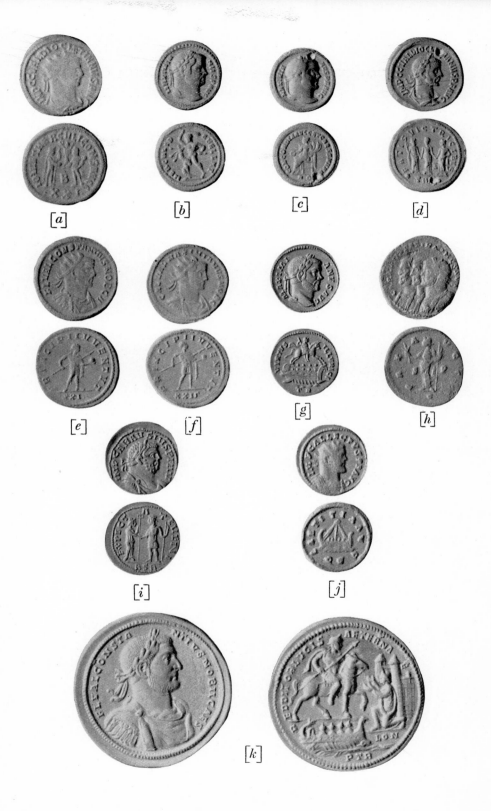

[a] [b] [c] [d]

[e] [f] [g] [h]

[i] [j]

[k]

COINS OF MAXENTIUS, CONSTANTINE, ALEXANDER, AND VALERIUS VALENS

[a] Aureus of *Alexander* minted at *Carthage*. Rev. INVICTA ROMA FEL. KARTHAGO, goddess of Carthage. (xii, 351.) [b], [c] *Maxentius*, bronze and silver. Revs. Temple of Roma, and She-wolf with twins. (xii, 351.)

[d] to [g] Aurei of *Constantine*. [d], [e] Rev. Sol, as the Emperor's comrade, holding a statue of Victory, a captive between them. (xii, 351, 680.) [f] Busts of Sol and the Emperor conjoined. Rev. Liberalitas. (xii, 351, 680.) [g] Rev. VBIQVE VICTOR, the Emperor between captives.

[h] Bronze of *Valerius Valens*. Rev. Juppiter Conservator. (xii, 692.)

[i], [j] Two bronze medallions minted under *Constantine* with busts of the City goddesses *Roma* and *Constantinopolis*. Revs. [i] The She-wolf and twins between shepherds, the stars of the Dioscuri above. [j] The Emperor as *Restitutor reipublicae* raising Tyche from her knees.

[*i, j* in *Berlin, c, d, f, g,* in the *British Museum,* the others in the *Bibliothèque Nationale, Paris*]

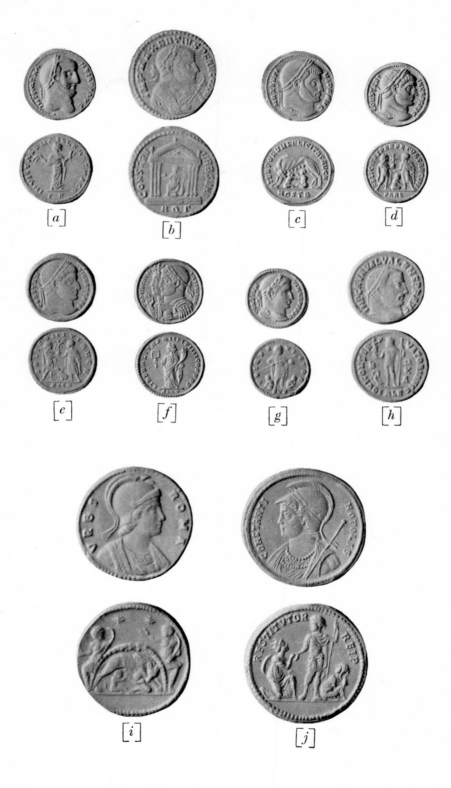

[a]   [b]   [c]   [d]

[e]   [f]   [g]   [h]

[i]   [j]